# FREE TO LOVE

# FREE TO LOVE

*Poverty – Chastity – Obedience*

## FRANCIS J. MOLONEY S.D.B.

Darton, Longman and Todd
London

First published in Great Britain in 1981
by Darton, Longman and Todd Ltd
89 Lillie Road, London SW6 1UD

© 1981 Francis J. Moloney, SDB

ISBN 0 232 51518 2

British Library Cataloguing in Publication Data

Moloney, Francis J.
  Free to love.
  1. Religious communities
  2. Christian life
  I. Title
  248.8'94        BX2435

ISBN 0–232–51518–2

Printed in Great Britain by The Anchor Press Ltd
and bound by Wm. Brendon & Son Ltd
both of Tiptree Essex

Who will deliver me from this body of death?
Thanks be to God through Jesus Christ our Lord!
There is therefore now no condemnation for those
who are in Christ Jesus. For the Law of the Spirit of
Life
in Christ Jesus has set me free from the law of sin and
death. (Romans 7:24–5; 8:1–2)

For freedom Christ has set us free; stand fast
therefore, and do not submit again to a yoke
of slavery. (Galatians 5:1)

# CONTENTS

# PREFACE

Earlier this year I published a major book on the Religious life entitled *Disciples and Prophets: A Biblical Model for the Religious Life* (London, Darton, Longman and Todd, 1980). The reaction to this book has been overwhelming. Reviewers in both Europe and Australia have been very enthusiastic about what I was trying to say there, and this has been a most encouraging experience. Above all, an extraordinary number of Religious have communicated, in various ways, their profound satisfaction with what I had attempted to say. Any author is encouraged when he finds that his efforts to give guidance and light to his readers have met with some sort of success, but with *Disciples and Prophets* there was more to it. In that book I struggled to find some sort of solution to a serious difficulty which, in my opinion, has bothered the Religious life since the Council. I would like to look briefly at this difficulty.

In the document on the Religious life, the Council Fathers insisted that one of the major criteria for the post-conciliar renewal was to be 'the following of Christ as it is put before us in the Gospel', and the document goes further to insist that this criterion 'must be taken by all institutes as the supreme rule' (*Perfectae Caritatis* 2). A glance back over the past fifteen years since the Council

will show that a great deal has been done to attend to the
various other criteria: a genuine study, understanding and
appreciation of the charism of each Religious family and
a healthily critical 'understanding of men, of the condi-
tions of the times and of the needs of the Church' (*Perfectae
Caritatis* 2). We have not always been successful in our
efforts in these areas, but serious and sustained attempts
have been made. What of 'the supreme rule': the following
of Christ *as it is put before us in the Gospel?* It is my
experience that insufficient attention has been given to this
central issue. There appear to me to be two reasons why
this is the case. First, the return to the charism of the
founder led us into all sorts of fascinating and enriching
historical and apostolic investigations; it was all so very
close to the surface and it posed such urgent demands
about what each Religious family was *doing* in the Church.
The same could be said of the reading of the signs of the
times. What must we *do* to play an actively effective role
among men and women in the Church and world of
today? These considerations are important, but they run
the danger of leading us away from the real issue: the
rediscovery of the person of Jesus of Nazareth, and the
setting out on a journey along his way. Secondly, we
seem to be frightened to read the Gospels because they
seem to belong to either the specialists, with all their
trappings of Greek, Hebrew and German scholarship on
the one hand, and the uncritical 'drop it open and let us
see what God is saying to us' attitude of certain enthusiastic groups on the other. It would be unfair to say that
all the fault lay on the side of the Religious themselves.
Far too often the people who have been given the opportunity to equip themselves for a serious and genuine understanding of the Gospels lose themselves in their
word-games and their tricks with literary techniques to
such an extent that they become irrelevant. None of this

is good enough! It appears to me that the next fifteen years of renewal in the Religious life must be dominated by a serious and sustained attempt to rediscover the Jesus of the Gospels, and to walk behind him, cost what it may. *Disciples and Prophets* was an attempt to contribute to such a rediscovery. As such, it was, for the author, far more than an academic exercise. It was my attempt to show how a serious and critical approach to the Bible produces a challenge to the Religious life which must be faced. I certainly make no claim to have provided all the answers, but following a general line already initiated by J. M. R. Tillard, O.P., and J. Murphy-O'Connor, O.P., I wished to raise the questioning finger of the Gospels yet again reminding myself, as well as my readers, of the age-old priority in an authentic Christian life: the supreme rule has always been and will always be 'the following of Christ as it is put before us in the Gospel' (*Perfectae Caritatis* 2).

As the reader will have gathered from the above, this is a matter of urgent and universal concern. However, a very practical factor has placed *Disciples and Prophets* outside the reach of the very people for whom it was written: each and every Religious, of whatever congregation, order, profession and skill. Despite the good will of my publishers, inflation and heavy duties placed the work among the books for the library shelf. This is not altogether a bad thing, and I hope and pray that it will find its place on those library shelves for the use and consultation of many. However, it left me restless as I still wanted to reach out to a wider audience, and a member of the Pauline family in Australia suggested that I try again. John M. Todd strongly supported that suggestion and the book which follows is the result of their insistence.

It is now almost two years since I submitted the manuscript of *Disciples and Prophets* to Darton, Longman and

Todd. In that period the story of those pages has been repeated time and again, but it never comes out exactly the same way. Each audience has its own sensitivity and the many searching questions aimed at me have repeatedly driven me back to the Gospels. Thus, although what follows is in many ways the central section of the longer book (pp. 85–129), it simply cannot be the same, 'For the word of God is living and active, sharper than any two-edged sword, piercing to the division of soul and spirit, of joints and marrow, and discerning the thoughts and intentions of the heart' (Heb. 4:12).

What I hope to present here is a reflection on the life of poverty, chastity and obedience, about which so much has been written over the centuries. Why another book? My reply is simply that I am not happy with what has been said in many of the classical treatises. The life of poverty, chastity and obedience is not an invention of fourth-century monks, laying the foundations for a certain state of life which has persevered in the Church down to our own time. It stands at the heart of the Gospel's radical demand that we walk behind the poor, chaste and obedient Jesus.

This leads me to one final consideration. In *Disciples and Prophets* I insisted that the Bible will allow of no superior class of Christians (see pp. 3–15). All are called to a perfection of love, and baptism inserts us *all* into the mystery of a Church and a life of Grace where this is rendered possible. Again the Council has made it clear:

> The Lord Jesus the divine Teacher and Model of all perfection, preached holiness of life to each and everyone of his disciples regardless of their situation . . . Thus it is evident to everyone that all the faithful of Christ *of whatever rank or status* are called to the *fullness* of the Christian life and to the *perfection* of Charity. (*Lumen Gentium* 40. Stress mine).

It is my opinion that we should not speak of Evangelical *Counsels*, as if they were something in the Gospels which may or may not be followed. Poverty, chastity and obedience are Gospel *imperatives* for all those who wish to follow Christ and thus enter into a new way of freedom for love, i.e. all the baptized. Naturally, there will be different *forms* of poverty, chastity and obedience, with the chastity of the celibate being the most striking of these. The biblical virtues of poverty, chastity and obedience are not the unique preserve of a small group of specialists in the Church, but they are the touchstone of true humanity, and thus of a true and authentic Christianity: the poor, the chaste and the obedient are freed to love and for love. As this is the case, it is my hope that the little book which follows may also fall into the hands of serious and questioning Christians of all walks of life. I am sure that they will find, *mutatis mutandis*, that the challenge of poverty, chastity and obedience issued by the Gospels strikes home. It must be so, as the Gospels were not written for Religious, but as a word of life to all those who claim to be followers of the poor, chaste and obedient Jesus of Nazareth.

I would like to thank the hundreds of Religious who have listened to what follows. God reveals himself among us in the human minds and hearts of men and women. I thank you all for what you have given me of your hearts and your minds. This book was written while at Oxford, catching again the tranquil atmosphere of a much-loved *Alma Mater* in the company of my Salesian confreres at Cowley. To that community I also owe much, and I would like to express my gratitude to them all, and especially Fr Bernard Higgins, S.D.B., for the friendship and support which I have always received here over the past eight years. Finally, I would like to thank a special person who stood by me faithfully as I once again went through the painful separation from those I love, amid all the trying circumstances and turmoil of August–September 1980. She knows the story – and to her, in thanks, I dedicate this book.

Salesian House
Cowley                      Francis J. Moloney, S.D.B.
Oxford OX4 2PE
St Francis of Assisi, 1980

# POVERTY

In my preface I stated that poverty, chastity and obedience were not counsels but imperatives, arising from the heart of the biblical message. However, a reading of the Old Testament seems to tell another story about poverty. In the greater part of the literature of the Old Testament poverty is seen as a curse, and the blessing of God was always judged in terms of material success and wealth. This was part and parcel of the concrete approach to life which was typical of the Hebrew people. They seemed to care little for the philosophical; if God was pleased with them, then he blessed them with material wealth, victory in battle and the many other blessings associated with a happy material life. The contrary was the case when he was angry with them. The book of Deuteronomy formulates this belief (see, for example, Deut. 7:6–26). There were many reasons for this, and perhaps the most important was the lack of any idea of an after-life in earlier Hebrew thought.

One of the most striking individual examples of this is found in the experience of Job. At the beginning of the book of Job he is described as a man 'who was blameless and upright, one who feared God, and turned away from evil' (Job 1:1). In this situation he is blessed with property, animals, household and a large family (see Job 1:3–5). However, all this is taken away from him, and Job con-

tinually sees this as evidence that God is displeased with
him, as also do his various interlocutors (see, among many
examples, Job 6:8–13; 8:2–7; 19:2–22). His anguish arises
from his inability to understand why God was so displeased. Through it all, he is faithful and at the end of the
book the Lord blesses him. It is important to notice that
the blessing of God is again measured in terms of material
abundance: 'The Lord restored the fortunes of Job . . .
and the Lord gave Job twice as much as he had before'
(42:10. See also verses 11–17).

Examples of this biblical attitude to wealth and possessions could be found throughout all the major books
in the Old Testament and it is an important corrective to
some of our current suggestions that the authentic form
of biblical poverty is to have nothing, to be reduced to a
state of total indigence. That is not the whole story.
Nevertheless, as Israel came to a political and religious
stage in her history when she was no longer master of her
own property, wealth and possessions, but when all of
the material side of her life seemed to be controlled by the
foreign powers whose vassal she was, a spiritualizing process began to take place. A most important part of this
stage of her history (after the return from the exile in 537
B.C.) was the gradual development of a belief in the
after-life. The inevitable question arose: why do the
wicked prosper and the virtuous starve? The answer had
to be that God's blessings and punishments could not be
measured by success or failure on this side of death. There
must be a final reward and punishment on the other side
of death. The most famous explicit confession of such a
belief is found in the well-known account of the slaying
of the mother and her seven sons in 2 Maccabees 7. The
second son defies his slayer with the words:

> You accursed wretch, you dismiss us from this present
> life, but the King of the universe will raise us up to an

everlasting renewal of life, because we have died for his laws. (2 Macc. 7:9)

After seeing the six older sons destroyed before her, the mother exhorts her youngest child:

Do not fear this butcher, but prove worthy of your brothers. Accept death, so that in God's mercy I may get you back again with your brothers. (2 Macc. 7:29)

This political and religious atmosphere created a parallel development in the thought of Israel. Now it was not the rich and the powerful who were blessed by God, for they were more often than not the violaters of God's law. It was the humble, the suffering and the poor who were to be blessed. They were called 'the poor of Jahweh', the *anawim*:

I will remove from your midst
your proudly exultant ones,
and you shall no longer be haughty
in my holy mountain.
For I will leave in the midst of you
a people humble and lowly.
They shall seek refuge in the name of the Lord,
those who are left in Israel;
they shall do no wrong
and utter no lies,
nor shall there be found in their mouth
a deceitful tongue.
For they shall pasture and lie down,
and none shall make them afraid. (Zeph. 3:11–13)

It is very important, for our purposes, to notice that this widespread belief in the blessedness of the poor and the humble (see, for example, Pss. 22:24; 40:17; 69:33; 86:1–2; 109:22) does not lie in the mere fact of their being poor and oppressed. They are promised that they will be freed from such a situation. Their blessedness is found in their complete and profound openness to Jahweh. In the light of their lack of political and economic power, they are freed to love, and in that love offered a blessed future which only Jahweh could offer: 'For they shall pasture and lie down, and none shall make them afraid' (Zeph. 3:13. See also Pss. 22:26; 40:17; 69:33; 86:12–13; 109:30–1).

This is the theme picked up in the New Testament, and especially by Luke, in its exaltation of 'poverty'. Mary, the mother of Jesus, is clearly presented as one of the *anawim*, as indeed are all the characters of the beautiful narrative of Luke 1—2: Zachariah, Elizabeth, Simeon and Anna. The theme is taken further into the preaching of Jesus. A few examples must suffice: the beatitudes (Luke 6:20–3), the invitation to the poor from the highways and the byways to the banquet (14:15–21), Luke's deliberate editing of Mark's passage on the radical nature of discipleship in 14:25–33, where he adds: 'So in the same way, none of you can be my disciple unless he gives up all his possessions' (v. 33, J.B.), and the story of the poor man Lazarus (16:19–31). However, it is not only Luke who has this idea; each one of the Gospels contains it in some way. The Marcan picture of Jesus is a powerful portrait of a man urgently pushing on to a destiny which leaves no time or opportunity for the gathering of possessions or the enjoyment of life's leisures, and Matthew, despite his differing point of view, continues in the same vein.

There can be little doubt that one of the impressions left by the historical Jesus was that of a man completely overpowered by the enormous 'riches' of the Kingdom of God. Here it was that he placed his trust, and this is the key to a correct understanding of the Gospel's message on poverty. However, I must not rush ahead. Central to the Christian ideal of poverty stands the story of the rich young man, and this account is found in all three synoptic Gospels (Mark 10:17–22; Matt. 19:16–22; Luke 18:18–23).

The tremendous ideal expressed in the words 'Go, sell what you have and give to the poor, and you will have treasure in heaven; and come, follow me' (Mark 10:21) stands at the heart of innumerable courageous attempts, down through the centuries of Christian history, to live a life of poverty. It has become the catch-word for what has been called 'evangelical poverty', and one of the basic elements within the structure of the Religious life.

It appears, therefore, that a life of poverty has ample support in the biblical tradition, in the life of Jesus, and in the history of Christian life. Our contemporary society, whose needs we must have continually in mind, also seems to be very open to some form of poverty. Given the affluence and the frantic search for the extra dollar this may appear to be a strange affirmation. However, one does not have to enquire very deeply to find that there is a dissatisfaction, both among the young and the not-so-young, with the slavery which our current search for material success is bringing about. Young people are destroyed as they reach beyond themselves; families are broken, as the search for that further advancement leaves love, hope and dreams out of the lives of people once full of love, hope and dreams. We live in a society which (to its detriment) often has little respect for the supposed 'dehumanising' effects of chastity or for certain forms of obedience and authority, but many are opting out of a system which is run by the very small number of financiers who ultimately decide what happens in a capitalist society. There is a growing sensitivity to the fact that true freedom will never be found in the world's attractive offer of wealth and possessions.

Within this context we must try to understand the practice of a vowed life of poverty in the Religious life. We have just seen that poverty has all sorts of support: it is biblically based, it appears to have been a part of the experience of Jesus, it has always been a part of the traditional structure of the Religious life in all its forms, and finally, it seems to provide an answer to some of the deepest and most sincere questions posed by contemporary men and women. Despite all of this, there can be little doubt that the practice of poverty in Religious life today gives rise to a great amount of division and bickering, and is the source of many practical problems. This is already a serious matter in itself, as it greatly lessens the witness value of the particular community in question, torn apart by the casuistry of how poverty should be lived. However, more serious than this is the anguish felt by a great number of sincere Religious who, struck by the suffering and pain of the impoverished millions of the world, and especially those who are being politically exploited, are often heard saying: 'We are not really poor. We have plenty to eat, cars to move about in, a roof over our heads and a warm bed every night. More than this, we are not powerless. We have means to fight our battles, and we are never exposed to the frightening insecurity about what "tomorrow" might bring. All of these things are part of the experience of poverty – but they are not part of my experience.' Although we have taken a vow of poverty, it appears that it would be preferable not to insist upon this aspect of our lives. Having all the things we have and being basically secure about our 'tomorrows' within a world-wide context of people who are not, it would appear foolish to argue that we are poor. How deeply it can hurt us when we hear that oft-repeated joke aimed at us by non-Religious: 'You take the vow of poverty – and we keep it!'

In the intense period of renewal which has gone on since Vatican II, this problem has become more and more urgent, and it has created many wonderful initiatives among Religious. But precisely because of a lack of serious consideration of what the Gospel has to say on the matter, I believe that a great deal of the anger, anxiety and confusion which we have all experienced was unnecessary. There seem to have been two major attempts to solve this problem which, stated in their extremes, could be formulated as follows:

1. To speak of a vow of poverty today makes no sense. What is demanded of us, if we wish to remain faithful to this aspect of the tradition, is that we give ourselves wholly and generously to the task to be done in the Church and in the world. One of the major catch-phrases which sums up this position is that poverty means *availability*. This infers that while we make our contribution to the Church and the world, we are free to live, on the material level, like any non-Religious doing the same work as ourselves. What will be outstanding in the life of the Religious will be his or her availability. This point of view has become, in fact, the practice of many Religious individuals and communities in the more economically stable societies of the United States, Great Britain and Australia.
2. In complete contrast to the solution just outlined, there is a growing insistence that we return to a literal observance of the radical command of Jesus to the rich young man: 'Go, sell what you have, and give to the poor' (Mark 10:21). This means that the Religious in the Church must make a definite option for the situation of the poor and the powerless, not just at the level of ideas, but at the level of practice. Large houses and the care and education of the wealthy must be abandoned; Religious communities must strip themselves of all worldly possessions and trappings, so that they may really share the experience of those who are poor, powerless and exploited. Especially important is the sharing of their insecurity. This attitude has been adopted in theory and in practice by Religious individuals and communities living in the difficult situations of South America.

One must be careful not to scoff and rule out either of

these attitudes (and the many variations and nuances of the same themes). There is much in them that can be of great value when it comes to the way in which some form of poverty has to be actually exercised. It may be true that we should be more careful in our use of the word 'poverty', since this word has taken on considerable political, social and even emotional implications in contemporary society which were never involved in the Latin *'paupertas'*, coined by the earliest reflections on the vowed life. It must also be said that availability has always been a most important aspect of the life of a committed Religious. It is certainly true that the urgent call to give power to the powerless and hope to the hopeless is a profoundly biblical call, and some of us may have to take the risk of sharing in the powerlessness and hopelessness on a material level in order to point to the Power and the Hope that can transform such situations. This is the lasting value of the message of the liberation theologians. Nevertheless, in my opinion, both of these solutions fail as the ultimate answer to the problem of the sense and function of poverty within the context of Christian and Religious life. These suggestions are not wrong because they are radical; the Christian vocation is a call to a radical and energetic living of Gospel values, and it is precisely here that I find the weakness. These suggestions have not gone far enough back into the true 'roots' of the Christian life. They have become bogged down in an attempt to find an immediate answer to the immediate problems of the confused world in which we live. As such, they are too obsessed with the questions of 'haves' and 'have-nots'. Ultimately, they are caught up in the casuistry of *how* it is to be done. The only possible way to a valid solution of the problem is to go back to the pages of the New Testament, to rediscover exactly what is demanded there. The solution which reduces poverty to availability fails because it loses touch with an integral part of the call to evangelize through a public commitment to a life consecrated to the biblical imperative of poverty, since availability can be found among many peoples and communities who lay no claim to be followers of Jesus. The second solution – 'Go, sell what you have and give to the poor' – also fails to be the complete answer, but here the deficiency is more subtle. It is my conviction that it fails because of a faulty interpretation of the New Testament, particularly the Lucan beatitudes (Luke 6:20: 'Blessed are you poor, for yours is the kingdom of God') and the story of the rich young man.

After this lengthy analysis of the situation, I must turn to a more detailed examination of the biblical texts, those just mentioned and others which must be seen as the biblical roots of the evangelical imperative of poverty.

## The Basic Premise: A Shared Life 'in Christ'

It is well-known that Paul devotes very little time and space to reflections on the person, personality and experience of Jesus of Nazareth. All we have is a note that he was 'born of a woman' (Gal. 4:4), that he instituted the Eucharist (1 Cor. 11:23–6) and that he died, was buried and rose again (1 Cor. 15:3–5). However, for Paul that is enough. The social and economic situation of Paul's communities is also rather difficult to discover from a reading of the letters. All we know is that the Jerusalem Church was struggling, thus the Pauline Churches contributed to a collection so that the original Church might survive (see 1 Cor. 16:1–4). The deeper significance of this Pauline concern will only be grasped later on in our considerations. Yet, despite Paul's clear design not to enter into casuistry until he has really spelt out the depths of the Gospel message, his development of that message is unavoidably linked with life and freedom. At the centre of Paul's gospel stands the story of a Jesus crucified but risen again. To everyone who is prepared to lose himself in love unto death, this Jesus offers a newness of life which can be ours now (see, for example, Rom. 5:1–5; Gal. 4:4–7) as we participate even on this side of death in what Paul calls 'life in Christ'. The concept of the Christian life being a 'life in Christ' dominates Paul's thought. From a reading of Romans alone, one can find almost every aspect of the Christian life described as 'in Christ'. The Christian is baptized 'in Christ' (Rom. 6:3), lives his everyday life, greets people, has his glory and the life of the Spirit 'in Christ' (Rom. 6:11; 8:2; 9:1; 15:17; 16:3–10), forms 'one body' with other Christians 'in Christ' (12:5) and has redemption and eternal life 'in Christ'. Although this may appear somewhat distant from the question of poverty, I hope that the reader will eventually come to see that it is the theological reality behind the Pauline expression 'in Christ' which stands behind any authentically biblical understanding of poverty.

Although there is some discussion among scholars as to what the expression 'in Christ' means for Paul, all are agreed that he uses it to communicate what he understands as the essence of Christian life. For Paul, to exist as a Christian, to 'be' a Christian in any active, serious way means to have one's life 'in Christ'. Here, therefore, we are in touch with an aspect of Pauline thought which is not just an interesting moral or even mystical reflection; we are at the heart of what it means to live as a Christian.

Perhaps the best way to understand what Paul means by 'in Christ', is to look at some of the texts where he uses it in association with some other famous images. Often Paul speaks of the Christian's 'putting on Christ' and his 'becoming a new man'. Again, we are not dealing with some sort of moral improvement or mystical experience; they are expressions used to describe the Christian's entering into a whole new way of *being* and *existing*. To be a Christian means that something radically new is happening. Just what is that newness? The answer to that important question is best expressed in two famous Pauline texts, where the images of 'in Christ', 'putting on Christ' and 'becoming a new man' are all used in close association with one another:

> As many of you as were baptized *into Christ* have *put on Christ.* There is neither Jew nor Greek, there is neither slave nor free, neither male nor female; for *you are all one in Christ Jesus.* (Gal. 3:27–8)

> You have *put on the new man . . . where* there cannot be Greek and Jew, uncircumcised and circumcised, barbarian, Scythian, slave, freeman, *but Christ is all in all.* (Col. 3:10, A.T.)

There are several important facts to be noticed about these two texts. They come from two quite different periods of Paul's life and are written within the context of two quite different experiences: Galatians is written with Paul in the full flood of his missionary activity, while Colossians is what is commonly called a 'prison letter', written toward the end of his career. As well as the difference in Paul's situation, they are written to two quite different communities, which had very different problems: the Galatian community was running the serious risk of turning back to the protection of the law and thus, according to Paul, losing their freedom (see Gal. 5:1), while the Colossians seemed to be facing problems from a more speculative, libertine, syncretistic stream of thought (see, for example, Col. 2:8–21). Despite these very important *differences*, the texts are clearly very *similar*. They share the list of traditionally hostile groups: Greek and Jew, circumcized and uncircumcized, slave and free-man, male and female. It is important to see the full meaning of what Paul is trying to say, to understand that these are *accepted* divisions. No one in his right mind would suggest that people should not be divided according

to that list – but Paul does! Both of these passages, reflecting a central idea in Paul's thought (see also Rom. 10:12–
13; 1 Cor. 12:12–13; Eph. 2:11–22), claim that these
accepted divisions are finished in an entirely new situation
into which the Christian has entered. This new situation
is described as 'in Christ', 'in the new man', and both the
Galatians and the Colossians are told that they have 'put
on Christ'. Notice also the idea of 'space'. In the passage
from Galatians Paul describes this new situation as a place
where all constitute 'one man', while in Colossians Paul
goes on further and explicitly says that 'the new man' is
a place *where* (Greek: *hopou*) there cannot be' such
divisions.

I hope that this fairly detailed analysis has made it clear
that 'life in Christ' is not a new set of moral habits. It is
clearly a new *sphere of existence*. To become a Christian in
a Pauline vision of things means to go away from one
*place* into another *place*, where all the normally accepted
barriers between men and women are brushed aside. All
of this has happened because of baptism into Christianity.
The Christian finds himself in an entirely new situation,
where others form an *integral* part. To spell this out more
clearly, the Pauline notion of life 'in Christ', Paul's central
understanding of what it meant to be a Christian, is
nothing less than an insistence that our very existence as
Christians is not something which we personally possess.
To be a Christian is to participate in the life of others, to
share, to break down all barriers which divide. It would
have been impossible for Paul to imagine an *autonomous*
Christian (of which we have so many today). For Paul,
autonomy and Christianity would be terms which contra-
dicted each other. We exist and have our life as Christians
*only* in our profound openness to the sharing of life and
love with other Christians. It is within this sphere of a

sharing of life, where all divisions are eliminated, that we can claim to be Christians.

A little reflection upon our own situations will show that it must be this way. Not one of us became a Christian, entered into the wonderful mystery of Church and the life of Grace, under our own steam! This was given to us by people who, in their own turn, drawn by the gift of God's love, were prepared to share what they already enjoyed: our parents or the people who drew us, by the quality of their own Christian lives of love, into this shared life 'in Christ'. Once we are 'in Christ', to abandon this shared life is to go 'out' of the life of Christ, it means an abandoning of Christianity, even if we were to have our private Mass and Communion and live according to the external observance of the commandments all our lives. I am not saying that such a person is not saved. That is another question. I am saying that he or she no longer enjoys the essence of the Christian life: life 'in Christ'. 'For freedom Christ has set us free; stand fast therefore, and do not submit again to a yoke of slavery' (Gal. 5:1).

This profound vision touches all aspects of the Christian life. No genuine Christian can live for himself because his very existence *as a Christian* would thus be lost to him. We have our Christian lives only in so far as we depend upon others, only in so far as we continually give to others and receive from others. We *are* Christians, we exist as Christians in, through, for and because of others. While the rest of the New Testament does not systematically work through a theology of 'life in Christ' as Paul does, the various authors simply presuppose such a life as their first premise. This can be seen in the extraordinary agreement in all the New Testament that there is only one law in Christianity: the new law of love. It had to be so, as to love and to allow oneself to be loved is the only way of human existence which makes possible 'life in Christ': to *be*, to exist for the other. This is the only way to authentic

Christian life: a mutual reciprocity and inter-dependence which Paul has called 'life in Christ'. Now that we have looked at the very roots of our Christian existence: a radical sharing of all that we are and all that we have, we can turn to examine some of the more classical passages in the New Testament which are used as the basis for discussions of a life of poverty.

## The Poverty of the Jerusalem Church

We have already seen that Luke's Gospel pays more attention to the question of the poor than the other Gospels. However, the author of the Gospel of Luke wrote a two-volume work, and the second volume is known to us as the Acts of the Apostles. Here, especially in the passages where the author is commenting or drawing his own conclusions (the scholars call them redactional passages) the concern with material goods continues. As this is the case, it has been traditional to look to the Lucan portrayal of the community gathered around Peter in Jerusalem reported in Acts 1—5. Before we analyze some of the passages from that section which seem to deal with the poverty of the Jerusalem Church, a few introductory remarks must be made. First, and most important of all, we must recognize that Luke is presenting the Jerusalem Church in these chapters as an ideal model for his own Church in the late seventies or the early eighties of the first century. There can be little doubt that Luke was depending upon some good sources for the basic facts of his report, but as he is using the Jerusalem Church as an ideal model for his own community, there can be little doubt that he has also idealized the situation there considerably. This leads me to my second introductory remark. The portrait of the Jerusalem Church was not written to be a model for Religious communities. Luke knew of no such phenomenon. He was using the Jerusalem Church as a model for his own local Church. The important theological message of peace, unity, love and a profound sharing at all levels, which is at the heart of Luke's message, is for the Church. Nevertheless, Religious communities are, in their own turn, 'Church'. We do not stand outside the universal Church; we belong to it and our communities must reflect the quality of a life of love which is demanded of the whole Church. Thus, not only am I permitted to use the model of the Jerusalem Church in my reflections, which are aimed primarily at the Religious life, I *must* use that model if I am to remain true to my basic insistence that *all* are called to the imperative of a perfection of love, be they Religious or non-Religious, priest, brother, sister or nun, married or unmarried.

We have just seen, from our study of the Pauline notion of life in Christ that the Christian is never a Christian on his own. Our very lives as Christians depend upon our preparedness to share life. It is most important to notice now that we are turning to the Acts of the Apostles, that even though Luke never tries to work this out systematically, he takes it as his basic point of departure. This can be seen immediately in two important passages, widely used to show the poverty of the Jerusalem Church.

> *And all who believed were together* and had all things in common; and they sold their possessions and goods and distributed them to all, *as any had need.* (Acts 2:44–5)

> *Now the company of those who believed were of one heart and soul*, and no one said that any of the things which he possessed was his own, but they had everything in common . . . *There was not a needy person among them,* for as many as were possessors of lands or houses sold them, and brought the proceeds of what was sold and laid it at the apostles' feet; and distribution was made to each, *as any had need.* (Acts 4:32–5)

There are three central issues to be noticed in these texts:

1. As I mentioned above, Luke presupposes a unity of love created by the new faith of the Jerusalem Church: 'and all who *believed* were *together*' (2:44); 'Now the company of those who *believed* were of *one heart and soul*' (4:32). Without this faith which produced a oneness among many, the rest of the passage would not make sense. Because the Christian faith of the community had produced a situation parallel to that described by Paul as 'life in Christ', the practical consequences flow logically.

2. Given the unity produced by faith, the first Christians did not rid themselves of all their wealth and possessions. They shared them! There is no suggestion in these texts that material things were intrinsically evil, and thus to be cast off if one wished to become holy. A careful and non-prejudiced reading of the passages makes it clear that what happened was a sharing of the many goods and possessions which belonged to various individual members of the community *to raise the standard of living of the needy members of the community* (see 4:34: 'There was not a needy person among them'). The handing in to the apostles of all that one might possess had nothing to do with a disdain for the value of material things. On the contrary, it was done to make sure of the comfort and material welfare of *all* the community. However, it must be stressed that the handing in of the goods was never an end in itself. What Luke is presenting here as the Christian ideal is not the handing in to some local Christian leader everything we possess, as if that was where Christian poverty found its solution. This *method* must not be made into an absolute. What is presented here has to be understood in the light of a faith which produces a unity of love: the earliest community shared all that it had as a sign of the love which each member of that community had for the others, especially those most in need. What is

described here, in fact, is a uniting love. Because they loved, they were prepared to share in the material goods of the community. The handing over of the goods thus becomes the visible, external world-questioning sign and gesture which points to a much deeper reality: the uniting and sustaining love which is the constitutive element in a Christian community – Paul's 'life in Christ'. In fact, it is not reported that the non-Christians of the first century A.D. said of the Christians: 'See how these Christians hand in their goods'. No, they were able to see through the external sign of the sharing of goods, and understand what was so startlingly new in a Christian community. They are reported to have said repeatedly: 'See how these Christians love one another!'

3. Clearly, the aspect just outlined must have made a profound impact upon the world which stood outside the community, and would then have become an important force in the process of evangelization. However, there would have been a further consequence which must have had a profound effect on the members of the community themselves. Given the fact that the goods were shared by all, everyone, including the wealthy, now depended on the community for their physical well-being. No longer do we have that situation of a subtle form of tyranny (so common among the many benefactors in contemporary society) where some (the wealthy) can dictate terms to the others (the poor) by giving to them – and thus binding them ever more tightly in the misery of their slavery. This form of sharing has nothing to do with the freedom which Christ has come to bring. The message from the Jerusalem Church is that *all* is *shared* by *everyone*. Again we find a practical situation which reflects – above all to those who are inside the community – the mutual interdependence and sharing at a deeper level of a 'life in Christ' which stands at the basis of Christian existence and authentic freedom for humanity.

From our analysis of these important texts, we can see that Christian poverty has three focal points:

1. It springs from a genuinely Christian existence, a life in Christ, where faith has produced a deep desire to love and to break down the barriers of disunity.
2. On a practical level, one places at the disposal of the community all that one has.
3. Finally, there is a shared responsibility for the material life of the community.

We have already examined the basic premise: life in Christ; we must turn now to give further consideration to the handing in of all and the sharing in the goods of the community.

## Giving the Community All that One Has

This aspect of Christian poverty is the one which causes most of us considerable difficulty. On the one hand, there is the tendency deep within each one of us to 'possess' – perhaps one of the most disastrous effects of sin in contemporary society. On the other hand, many of us feel uncomfortable when we are faced with the proposal mentioned earlier: the *only* way to true Christian poverty is to follow to the letter the words of Mark 10:21: 'Go, sell what you have, and give to the poor'. Right from the start one fact should be made clear. For the New Testament, in fact for the whole of the Bible, complete personal deprivation, the lack of any means of subsistence, is *not* a good thing. The healthy attitude to God's blessings and subsequent material comfort as it is presented in the earlier books of the Old Testament are not without value, and should not be forgotten. How is it possible to find in the Gospels praise for hunger and starvation, malnutrition, exploited and powerless peoples? All of this is a contradiction of the nature of the Kingdom of God, continually

presented as the active reigning presence of a God who
loves, as a place full of joy, peace, love, warmth, and
where man is able to live with the dignity which is his
because he is the creation of a loving, caring God. Indeed
man is the very image of that God (see Gen. 1:26). The
Bible speaks of freedom for the captives, health for the
sick, and the images of wedding feasts and a superabund-
ance of wine, food and all good things are used (see, for
example, Amos 9:13; Hos. 14:7; Jer. 31:12; Mark 2:22;
Matt. 8:11; 22:1–14; Luke 22:16–18). How then have we
come to the position, standing at the heart of that nagging
feeling of guilt, that disturbs so many sincere Religious,
that we are not evangelically poor? As I have already
suggested, this difficulty flows from a mistaken interpretation of the Gospels, especially the Beatitudes and the
story of the rich young man.

*The Beatitudes*
The Beatitudes have come down to us in two quite different versions, in Luke 6:20–3 and Matt. 5:3–10. Although both versions reflect the interests and the literary
skill of the Evangelists, it is generally agreed that the form
of these words of Jesus is much closer to the original in
Luke than in Matthew. Luke's linking of the under-privileged with the Kingdom is immediate and urgent, while
Matthew tends to soften this somewhat. The Lucan Beatitudes promise a fulfilment which the messianic era will
bring for the under-privileged:

> Blessed are you poor, for yours is the Kingdom of God.
> Blessed are you that hunger now, for you shall be
> satisfied.
> Blessed are you that weep now, for you shall laugh.
> (Lk. 6:20–1)

This passage is often read as a beatification of the state
of being poor and oppressed; only to people who are

suffering in this way is the Kingdom of God promised.
Nothing is said of others. This is a misreading of the text
and a misplacing of the emphasis, and such an interpretation can only come about when the text is pulled out
from the overall message of the Bible as a whole, and
Luke's general argument in particular.

The Messiah was not coming to establish a situation of
poverty, hunger and tears. That would be to make nonsense of the whole of the Bible. The Messiah was expected
to free men and women from such situations. This is a
common theme in the Old Testament, and Luke continues
that tradition. In Luke's Gospel (and *only* in Luke's Gospel)
Jesus' first public act, in the synagogue at Nazareth, is to
proclaim that he has come to fulfil the messianic expec-
tations of Israel. Quoting from Isa. 61:1–12 and Zeph. 2:3,
he announces:

> He has anointed me to preach good news to the poor.
> He has sent me to proclaim release to the captives
> and recovery of sight to the blind,
> to set at liberty those who are oppressed. (Luke 4:18)

Jesus claims that he comes as the anointed one of God,
the Christ who has come not to bless poverty, hunger and
tears, but to release people from these sufferings.

If that is the case, what are we to make of the promise
of the Beatitudes? Precisely because people are poor, hungry and in tears, the Messiah will release them. Do they
have any special privileges? Indeed they do. What is needed for the redemption which Jesus came to bring is a
complete and radical openness to the word and person of
Jesus of Nazareth. Here it is that the poor, the hungry and
the afflicted have an advantage: they are the ones who will
welcome him. These are the people who will gladly welcome the Kingdom announced by Jesus, because they have
no reason to defend the *status quo*. They will not react
against the searing, questioning words of Jesus to protect

their personal interests, because they have none! They are
not happy with the *status quo* and thus they make ideal
men and women of faith. They possess that basic discontent with the present which is a necessary pre-requisite for
faith. Without such a discontent we rapidly settle for what
we have here and now, and there is no openness to a new
future. The Christian faith must always be a 'walking
behind' Jesus of Nazareth, as he leads us further and further away from ourselves into the mystery of an Exodus
God. It can never be a sitting down to be comfortable and
happy with what we have under our control.

What is blessed in the Lucan beatitudes is not material
poverty, despite the use made of this passage by some
contemporary writers. The poor, the hungry and the
afflicted are blessed because they possess the one true possession: a radical openness to a new future which is char-
acteristic of the poor. It must be stressed that material
'having nothing' is never a biblical virtue in itself. It is
blessed because it creates an openness which is the source
of true blessing – an openness to a future which only God
can create. We should be warned against the faulty linking
of blessedness with the state of poverty by the third
Beatitude:

'Blessed are you that weep now, for you shall laugh'
(Luke 6:21). Those who weep are not only the poor, but
they are also promised the joys of the Kingdom. They too
are open to a new possibility. This is not to theorize, as
we all know the tragedy and anguish which more often
than not strikes at the hearts of the wealthy. These situations are real possibilities for faith, and thus for the inbreak
of the Kingdom. In the midst of their tears, the wealthy
can be forced to their knees as it is brought home to them
that they cannot control their ultimate hopes, plans and
longings by their purse strings or their influential contacts.
All of this is vain. *In itself* possession of wealth need not
be an obstacle to the possession of the Kingdom, even

though in many cases it may prove to be so. What must be seen here, however, is that the Lucan Beatitudes offer no biblical grounds for the all too common link which is made between material indigence and the following of Jesus. The contrary, however, is still maintained, largely because of the misinterpretation of the story of the rich young man.

## The Story of the Rich Young Man

This story comes to us in each of the synoptic Gospels but there are really only two versions. Mark (10:17–22) is largely followed by Luke (18:18–23) with only a few stylistic changes, but Matthew has reworked the Marcan story to introduce a theology of 'perfection' which is very important to his overall argument (Matt. 19:16–26). I will briefly analyze the Marcan story, adding a few remarks on the Matthean version where necessary. All the Evangelists present the man as a wealthy person who has administered his wealth with justice. In fact, only Matthew (19:20) refers to him as a 'young man'. For Mark (10:17) he is simply 'a man' and for Luke (18:18) he is 'a ruler'. I will continue to refer to the story of the rich young man as it is immediately recognized by that title. The first thing Jesus does is to test his justice according to the Law of Israel. That is the point of the list of commandments which Jesus asks him to observe (Mark 10:19; Matt. 19:18–19; Luke 18:20). It is important to notice that only those commandments which deal with his treatment of his neighbour are put to him. These are the commandments which a proud rich man would be most likely to offend, while he may have all the externals of the ritual observance of his duties to cult and observance in perfect order. On hearing from the man that he has always observed these commandments, 'Jesus looking upon him loved him' (Mark 10:21). The man has shown a deep desire to go further than he has gone through his observance of the commandments and Matthew makes a great deal of this, placing on the lips of Jesus the words, 'If you wish to be perfect' (Matt. 19:21) and then taking up the Markan condition for discipleship, 'Go, sell what you have, and give to the poor, and you will have treasure in heaven; and come, follow me' (Mark 10:21; Matt. 19:21; Luke 18:22). This is the radical demand which has inspired many generous and courageous hearts to extraordinary and great initiatives but these wonderful examples must not block us from asking the central question of the passage. Clearly the man is being called to discipleship, and Matthew here and elsewhere (see Matt. 5:48) has called that life a life of perfection, which reaches beyond anything that the observance of the Law can offer. The question which should be posed is: must this request be made of everyone who wishes to be a disciple of Jesus? Is it a universal law of the Gospel that *only* those who sell everything and give to the poor can become disciples of Jesus?

Strangely enough, a study of all the other vocation stories in the Gospels shows no trace of this. In Mark 1:16–20, the fishermen do abandon their nets, their boats, their hired servants and their father. In Mark 2:14 Levi does abandon his position in the taxhouse, but there is no command to poverty, nor is there any indication that all had to be sold up so that the proceeds could go to the poor. In fact, on a practical level, this would be pointless, as the rich would become poor and the poor rich, and thus the vocation of the poor would be lost. That, of course, is to make nonsense of the story. In fact, according to John 21:1–14, the same disciples return to the lake, to their boats and to their fishing after the death of Jesus.

What then is the point of the radical condition for discipleship which Jesus aims at the rich young man? Why is this particular demand made of this particular man and of *no one else* in the gospel traditions of the vocation to discipleship? The answer is to be found in the self-confi-

dent request of the man himself, found in all three versions
of the story (Mark 10:17; Matt. 19:16; Luke 18:18). 'What
must *I do* to inherit eternal life?' Here we have a man who
is used to deciding his own destiny, because he has the
power (notice Luke's description of him as 'a ruler') and
the wealth to force the issue. As we have just seen from
our analysis of the Beatitudes, this is not the way of faith.
He must be reduced to a situation where all that matters
is what the Lord can do for and with him. Thus Jesus, in
calling him to discipleship, must strip away all that stands
between the man and a radical commitment to himself.
*In the case of this man*, it is his wealth. He is blocked from
a total commitment to Jesus because he wants to control
his own future, as he always has. Thus, the means he has
at his disposal to dictate such terms must go! The story
is ultimately about the radical nature of true faith. All that
stands between the believer and an unconditional surren-
der of self to Jesus must be stripped away. The story is
*not* a universal call to all who would wish to become
disciples of Jesus to reduce themselves to a state of financial
indigence. That is to universalize the wrong issue. The
question of possessions is *this man's* problem. What is of
universal significance is the need to shed all pretensions to
power, to shake off the desire to dictate terms in the
Kingdom, to rid ourselves of anything which stands between ourselves and a radical *following* (never leading) of
Jesus of Nazareth.

There is a similar story, with the same call to radical
faith in Matt. 8:21–2. In a context dealing with discipleship
(see vv. 18–27) we find the following: 'Another of the
disciples said to him, "Lord, let me first go and bury my
father." But Jesus said to him, "Follow me, and leave the
dead to bury their own dead." ' Thank goodness we have
had the common sense not to universalize the detail of
that particular story. As with the rich young man, between this disciple and Jesus stands an obstacle. However,

in this case it is not wealth, but an affective relationship. It has to go! As can be clearly seen, both stories are concerned with the radical nature of authentic faith. Wealth and affective relationships can block our commitment to Jesus, but these accounts must never be taken as a gospel message that *only* those who are economically underprivileged and *only* those without attachment to their families, their father, mother, wife, husband and children can become disciples of Jesus. That would be to make the gospel message quite irrelevant to the major part of humanity, and to make a lie out of our experience of life and love among those very people from whom we have all learned most about the following of Jesus of Nazareth.

Returning, however, to the true roots of our Christian existence, our life 'in Christ', we can see that, somehow, these accounts do apply to our poverty. We have seen from our analysis of the passages from Paul and the Acts of the Apostles that our poverty is never an end in itself. It is an expression of a deeper reality: the profound desire to share all that we have and all that we are because of the unique experience of our faith in Christ Jesus. Our lives of poverty, where all is given, announce to the world, not the evil of possessions, but the value of a shared life inspired by the radical faith demanded from the rich young man. This shared life is outwardly reflected in the sharing of all that we are and all that we have, and it must make the world stop and wonder what makes us live this way. The answer must not be phrased in terms of economics or sacrifice, but in terms of that extraordinary gift which is ours: the sharing of a new life in Christ.


## A Shared Responsibility for the Material Life of the Community

I would like to point out once again that all that we have seen so far is not exclusive to the Religious life. In one form or another, it is the vocation of all the baptized. This final section must also be seen in the same fashion, but as I will be now looking into more practical questions, I will have to limit myself to the way in which this New Testament notion of a shared life works itself out in the practice of the life of a vowed community in such a way that it proclaims to the world what 'life in Christ' can really mean.

It stands to reason that no community (Religious or not) can survive unless each one of the members assumes an *active* responsibility for the other members. If our Christian existence depends upon our readiness to share at all levels, in the simplest and in the deepest of our affairs, then all of us, in some way or other, must be productive. Primarily, each one of us must generate the faith, the hope and the love which sustains others. There is little need to dwell here on the numerous examples of this which can be found in almost every Religious community: the smiling face of the infirm, elderly confrere who makes the struggling youngster see that, somehow, all this makes sense. Far too often, Religious fail to see the enormous witness value of this genuine sharing of life which we merely accept and enjoy. It is a vital part of our lives vowed to poverty. A similar productivity is also required from us at the level of material goods. This is where the notion of poverty as 'having nothing' falls short of the Christian ideal. None of us – no matter how aged, infirm or incompetent – has nothing. Each one of us is a unique creation of God, and this flows into what we do. Not all are 'gifted', in the narrow sense that the world gives to this term, but what we are is reflected in what we do, however modest that may be.

The idea that poverty is to have nothing and to wait for God to send bread from heaven has been seen as what the Gospels demand. I have insisted that this is to misunderstand the Gospels. In reality, it can often lead to a

bone-lazy materialism, especially in some countries where
the priests, brothers and 'the poor sisters' will never be
left without, as they are surrounded by an adoring laity
which considers itself as second class, and which subcon-
sciously feels that some holiness will rub off if they as-
sociate with the Religious, the first-class citizens of the
Kingdom. No Christian and therefore no Religious is
called to live off his local community.

A look at the history of Religious life shows that right
from the start communities have seen it as their responsibility to work for their own needs. Pachomius, the founder of the cenobitic life, hired himself and his monks out
to work in the fields during the harvest season and Basil
the Great demanded that all his monks have a trade. The
name that comes to mind immediately as an objection is
that of Francis of Assisi, so often romanticized in this
connection. In fact, he was proud to earn his living and
ordered his followers to continue the trades which they
had practised before they came to him. It is important to
know that he permitted them to beg only when there was
no work, or when the salary was not enough to live on
(*Regula Prima* 7; Test. 19–22).

The people among whom we live and for whom we
work *see us* at work and this is where we have to pose
them questions. What I have written so far could be mis-
understood, as if I were arguing that our poverty began
and ended with work. We do *not* exist so that we may
work. On the contrary! Our work points to *the reason why
we exist as a consecrated Christian community*. We must question the values of the world by causing them to ask why
talented, professional, hard-working (or not so talented,
professional and hard-working) people, all work and live
together, often in close contact with conflicting person-
alities, in and for a concrete, historical community. The
witness value of our poverty does not lie in our parading
through the streets with the soles of our shoes flapping off

or our elbows showing through our jackets. That sort of thing may raise eyebrows, but it does not command respect – much less imitation, and ultimately our most effective form of evangelization is the love and unity of our lives together. Our poverty calls us to a radical sharing of all that we are and all that we have, so that we may produce a quality of community life that makes people stop and wonder. When the world sees that all our efforts are directed, not to personal aggrandizement but to the support and strengthening of our life in Christ, then we may be seen as 'world stoppers', questioning the futile values that the world creates when it makes a god of personal success and material values.

## The Function of the Vow of Poverty Today

Poverty is not about being freed from financial worries so that we may work more effectively; it is about being freed for love. It is about showing the world, through the radical sharing of all that we have, that we also share all that we are, in our shared life of faith 'in Christ'. This must work itself out in the context of material things and can be formulated simply as: all that I have I give *to* the community, all that I need, I receive *from* the community. All that I am I give *to* the community, all my support I receive *from* the community. Living in this way, each member of the community knows and experiences that the responsibility for the material well-being of the community lies with all the members and not just with the ones whose task it is to keep the books! However, this shared responsibility on a material level is nothing if not the external sign of the love which should unite a Christian community.

All Christians are called by the Gospels to a radical sharing of all that they have and all that they are and hope to be. My analysis of the material from the New Testament has shown this. The message of the Gospel is clear: all men should have the possibility of becoming all that God made them to be. To make this possible, all are called to a radical sharing, if they profess the faith of the Gospels. This, ultimately, was the sense of the sharing that went on in the apostolic community: 'There was not a needy person among them' (Acts 4:34).

The signs of our times show that the world, and possibly the Christian Church, seem to have lost touch with this radical call to evangelical poverty. We see a Christian Europe and a Christian North America living with an easy conscience beside Africa and South America. But these are the immediately obvious examples of the scandal of contemporary Christian society. Closer to home, in each village and hamlet, society is clearly divided between those who have, and those who do not have. As management locks itself in bitter struggle against a protesting, striking work-force, no one seems to recognize that all this strife is nothing more than a subconscious screaming out that man was not made to live in this way. These divisions are also found within the confines of the confessing Christian churches, where wealth of possessions and culture in one community can live side by side with terrible poverty in another. This sort of division makes a lie out of the same Gospel which *both* the communities *preach*. They are called to *live* that Gospel.

In this situation the challenge of Religious poverty, which is a radical sharing of all that we have and all that we are, takes on a prophetic function. The Religious community has publicly committed itself to showing, by the quality of its shared life, that true humanity, and thus true Christianity, is not just a *preached* message, but a lived reality *within the Church*, and fired by the same ideals which fire the whole Church. The vow of poverty is not an end in itself. It is a major aspect of our prophetic function within the Church, showing the Church and the

world that it is only through the freedom won by a radical
observance of evangelical poverty that we can ever hope
to love as Christ loved.


## Conclusion

We must try to avoid a hard and fast definition of the
*things* which make for poverty. This will necessarily vary.
It should be a matter of plain common sense that the
material context of no two communities (even in the same
city) is the same. There can be no universal list of what
we can have or not have; what matters is that our difference, from the slavery of the world to personal achieve-
ments on the material plane, be *visible*. This necessarily
puts us within the context of material things, but they are
not the ultimate measure of our poverty – our shared life
'in Christ' is. We cannot confine this to intellectual and
practical criteria. Subtly, to allow these lists is to submit,
like the rest of society which we are trying to question,
to the criterion of materialism itself. The roots of our
poverty cannot and must not be intellectualized, because
the reciprocal dependence and productivity, at all levels,
which are the essence of the vow of poverty, cannot be
intellectualized and made into a list of things. It acquires
its value only if it is motivated by love of an exceptional
quality.

Reasons can always be found for a list of 'do's' and
'don'ts' or 'may-haves' and 'may-not-haves', but if we are
honest, we must admit that the need for such lists in our
community reflects a rather painful truth. The reality of
our life together, the quality of our shared life in Christ,
is often very poor, and thus we rush to create structures,
to draw up lists which will convey (primarily to ourselves,
because others are generally not fooled) an external sign
that we are poor. The problem with this system, however,
is that the self-centred, non-sharing member of a com-

munity can be 'perfect' in matters of poverty, while all sense of true biblically-based poverty has been lost, and the community divided.

Genuine love, the self-sacrificing love of Christ, cannot be measured by laws and lists, as it goes beyond any sort of material measurement. Our vow of poverty is one of our major means of showing to the world that we are committed to this love and when we examine our consciences on poverty we must start at the level of our shared life of love, and only when we have come to grips with this basic motive for our very existence as a Christian community should we turn our attention to the material circumstances which are only the context within which our poverty, our shared life 'in Christ', must work itself out.

# CHASTITY

There has been an unfortunate tendency among some contemporary writers on the Religious life and the vows to single out the chastity of the Religious as the unique distinguishing feature of this form of life within the Church. It is unique because in Religious life men and women consecrate themselves to chaste celibacy. In fact, several authors and indeed several congregations in their post-Vatican-II constitutions, have moved away from the traditional form and order of poverty, chastity and obedience to speak and write of celibacy, poverty and obedience. It appears to me that this is an unhealthy step. We must give full recognition to 1,600 years of tradition, where this aspect of the vowed life of the Religious has always been called 'chastity'. As this is the case, then there must be very good reasons for such a tradition. The reason is near at hand. I have insisted several times that we should not speak of Evangelical Counsels, but of Evangelical Imperatives – aimed at all those who are committed to following Jesus of Nazareth. With poverty and obedience this is fairly obvious, but it is extremely important for us to understand that all Christians, celibate or married, are called to chastity. In fact, most Christians live a vowed form of chastity. Some of us publicly profess this vow and commit ourselves to a Religious community, where we attempt to live the high ideals of a celibate form of

chastity. Others publicly profess it in the marriage cere-
mony and commit themselves to a husband or a wife in
the equally demanding ideal of the chastity found in faithful and fruitful conjugal love.

We will be concerned with the celibate form of chastity
in the pages that follow, but I hope that the reader will
sense throughout the analysis of the conciliar and biblical
material that what the Gospels say to us about celibate
love applies powerfully to conjugal love. For too long
these two forms of the same commitment to chastity have
been seen in a contrasting fashion, as far too much stress
has been given to their physical aspects. Celibacy is a
physical state; it is not a theological virtue. We must resist
any tendency to reduce this vow to a physical state. We
are vowed to chastity, and there are a great number of
celibates who are not chaste, while there are many non-
celibates whose chastity is outstanding. There are various
pastoral and practical consequences which flow from these
important reflections, but they will be touched upon later.

## The Objections to Chastity

We are all well aware of the series of objections that are
put to a life of chastity from a secularized world which
uses sex to add colour and interest to even the most innocent human interests and pastimes. A few hours in front
of a television set will teach us all we need to know about
these objections. I have no desire to lament these problems, but it is precisely to this heavily sexualized world
that our lives should speak. We will never convert the
world by talking about chastity unless our lives continually make people wonder if, perhaps, they have not
somehow gone wrong. Within this section my concern is
to show that today there are serious objections to chaste
celibacy which arise from within a Christian view of
things.

The Second Vatican Council, for the first time in the history of the Church, made its own two very important new teachings which seriously question some of the traditional motives for chaste celibacy. I must stress here, however, that both of these teachings did not simply fall out of the heavens at the Council. They were merely the final magisterial articulation of theological reflection which had been widespread in the Church for the greater part of this century.

The first of these new teachings concerned the salvific value of created reality. As a traditional spirituality attempted to show the value of chastity, there was a tendency to play down all that was natural, and man's being supernatural was seen as best expressed by his being chaste. This led to an under-valuation and, at times, a rather negative view of all that was natural and physical, and it was in this view of things that the celibate state was spoken of as 'angelic' and the better way, as it was the more spiritual way. Against this tendency, Vatican II devoted a chapter of its decree on the Church in the Modern World to man's activity within the context of created reality (*Gaudium et Spes* 33–9). The role of created reality in the plan of God was beautifully expressed as the Church proclaimed:

> If by the autonomy of earthly affairs is meant the gradual discovery, exploitation and ordering of the laws and values of matter and society, then the demand for autonomy is perfectly in order: *it is at once the claim of modern man and the desire of the creator.* By the very nature of creation, material being is endowed with its own stability, truth and excellence, its own order and laws . . . Believers, no matter what their religion, have always recognised the voice and the revelation of God in the language of creatures. (*Gaudium et Spes* 36; the stress is mine)

Men and women are not saved *despite* their belonging to
the world of material things, *despite* the fact that they are
flesh and blood, and therefore sexual beings, but *because
of it*, and in and through their being situated in God's
creation.

A second very important teaching from Vatican II
which is closely related to what we have just seen is a
magnificent presentation of the sanctity of the married
state, and the sanctification which comes to the married
through a life of faithful gift of self in conjugal love. Here
the teaching Church leans heavily on the Scriptures and
especially on Eph. 5:21–3:

> Just as of old God encountered his people with a cov-
> enant of love and fidelity, so our Saviour, the Spouse
> of the Church, now encounters Christian spouses
> through the Sacrament of marriage. He abides with
> them in order that by their mutual self-giving spouses
> will love each other with enduring fidelity, as he loved
> the Church and delivered himself for it. Authentic mar-
> ried love is caught up into divine love and is directed
> and enriched by the redemptive power of Christ and
> the salvific action of the Church. (*Gaudium et Spes* 48)

There are two very important points to be noted here.
There is a wonderful parallel drawn between the gift of
Jesus in his sacrifice of self for the Church and the 'mutual
self-giving' of married couples. That very aspect of marriage which is so abused and debased by contemporary
culture, and which has been somewhat frowned upon in
certain areas of Christian spirituality is paralleled (following Eph. 5:21–3) with the most wonderful moment in the
history of God's relationship with man: Christ's gift of
himself for us. Then there is that final statement that, in
a situation of 'authentic married love' we have the revelation of God's love reflected in the redemptive power of
Christ at work in their lives. This is in no way a

'second-class' citizenship in the Kingdom. It is a wonderfully privileged place among men where a God who is love is revealed, and where men and women can find an exquisite means of sanctification.

If this is the case with the vow of chastity and the practice of faithful conjugal love in marriage, what is the place of the vow of chastity and the practice of celibate love in the Religious life?

## The Traditional Case for Celibate Chastity

The Church has always seen virginity as having a special place among Christians. It appears that the saying about being 'eunuchs for the sake of the Kingdom of heaven' in Matt. 19:12 is a gospel passage which shows the superiority of virginity and Paul certainly advises the Corinthians that if they are not married they would do well to remain so: 'to secure your undivided devotion to the Lord' (see 1 Cor. 7:32–5). The early centuries of the Church saw a great concentration on the state of virginity, and the writings of the Fathers of the Church certainly reflect an underlying feeling that baptism and marriage go together rather uncomfortably. Perhaps the greatest of the Fathers, St Augustine, is the best-known example. In trying to explain, in his struggle against Pelagius, that infants needed Grace, he had to solve the problem of how an innocent child could be 'of the world' and not 'of Christ'. Augustine argued, correctly, that no one could save himself by his own efforts, but that we were all in need of the saving intervention of God's Grace in our lives. Pelagius countered this argument by asking how an innocent child, newly-born and never having committed sin, needed the Grace of Christ. Augustine struggled for a long time with this problem, but his final solution was that essential to the conception of a child, even among Christian married couples, was concupiscence. All children are born within the context of a physical desire, concupiscence, and thus do not belong to God but to the world: 'Because of this concupiscence it comes to pass that even from just and rightful marriages of the children of God, not children of God but children of the world are born' (*De nuptiis et concupiscentia* I, 18, 20).

Augustine must be understood within his own historical context (he tended to react very strongly against his former way of life as a Manichean) and within the context of the overall argument which he is pursuing. His basic argument was extremely positive. He insisted upon a universal need for the Grace of Christ, and the discussion about infants arose only within this context. Nevertheless, Augustine still reflects the negative stance already taken by some of the earlier Fathers, and this generally felt view of marriage became rather fixed in tradition, although it never became a part of church teaching. Very emphatic were the ideas of a man like Tertullian whose hard line on matters of sexual activity and marriage eventually led him out of the Church into a heretical sect, the Montanists (in A.D. 211–12), who had equally negative views on marriage and sexual activity. Given the widespread favour which these opinions had in the early centuries (although few were as extreme as Tertullian) it is remarkable evidence of the guidance of the Spirit in the Church that such positions *never* became part of the official teaching, even though traces of it creep into some lesser legislation.

It is clear that a certain interpretation of Matt. 19:12 and 1 Cor. 7:32–5, along with the consistent teaching of the Fathers of the Church have been very influential in the formation of a certain line of argument to defend the place of virginity in Christian tradition. Contemporary historical criticism is questioning the value of both of the sources for this longheld view. As we shall see, it is possible that Matt. 19:12 has nothing to do with the chastity of some who commit themselves to a vowed life of celibacy. St

Paul's teaching in 1 Cor. 7 is very heavily influenced by his belief that the end time was to come very soon, a belief which proved to be wrong, and thus his argument loses its force. There is also a widespread insistence that we understand the Fathers of the Church within the context of their times. The early Church unconsciously reflected the decadent late-Roman world in its over-reaction to the problems of sexual licence and it is also important to understand how their theology of virginity is closely linked to, and a continuation of, the theology of martyrdom. In the first two centuries of the Christian Church's existence martyrdom loomed large in her life. The earliest writers of the Church necessarily faced this problem and wrote beautifully of its significance for an authentic life of discipleship; when the phenomenon of martyrdom lessened, this theology passed easily into the reflections of the Fathers upon a life of virginity. As we shall see later, this was a valuable contribution to the growth of the Church's thought, but we must be careful not to *universalize* the Fathers' teaching on virginity. It appears, therefore, that we must look again at our sources and see if a helpful, guiding teaching on the sense and purpose of a vow of chastity can be discovered.

## Vatican II

Given the beautiful teaching which came from Vatican II on the holiness of the chaste life of conjugal love, we have every right to look to the teaching of the Church for guidance about a contemporary answer to the problems which a life of vowed chaste celibacy poses, from a Christian point of view. This question is dealt with explicitly in the document on the Renewal of Religious life:

Chastity 'for the sake of the Kingdom of heaven' (Matt. 19:12) which religious profess, must be esteemed an exceptional gift of grace. It uniquely frees the heart of man (cf. 1 Cor. 7:32–5), so that he becomes more fervent in love for God and for all men. For this reason it is a special symbol of heavenly benefits, and for religious it is a most effective means of dedicating themselves wholeheartedly to the divine service and the works of apostolate. (*Perfectae Caritatis* 12)

The Religious, having read of the wonders of married love in *Gaudium et Spes* 48, has every right to feel a little disappointed with this treatment of his life of celibacy. The number goes on with a series of warnings:

Religious, at pains to be faithful . . .
they should not presume on their own strength . . .
they should practise mortification and custody of the senses.
Nor should they neglect the natural means which promote health of mind and body.
They should not be influenced by false doctrines.
Candidates ought not to go forward . . . except after really adequate testing . . .
warned against the dangers to chastity.

I am not saying that any of this is wrong, but we may have expected something a little more positive! This general atmosphere of danger, caution and fear does not help us a great deal in our attempt to formulate and live a positive and joyful theology of chastity.

However, I find this number of *Perfectae Caritatis* misleading on a far more important issue than its negative tone. Taking up the tradition, the Council has used Matt. 19:12 and 1 Cor. 7:32–5, interpreting these texts to mean that chastity 'frees the heart of man', and thus is 'a most effective means of dedicating themselves wholeheartedly to the divine service and the works of the apostolate'. The document goes on to speak very well of a chaste life being a wonderful eschatological 'sign', and this is very true, but the idea conveyed in the first part of the number is plainly that chastity is a means by which the Religious is freed from the encumbrance of a family so that he or she may be able to work and pray more effectively. I believe that this is to misinterpret the biblical evidence used (Matt. 19:12 and 1 Cor. 7:32–5), but it also poses a problem at a practical level. If the chaste celibate is able to come closer to God in work and prayer because of his celibacy, where does that put the chaste married person? We must be logical and conclude that their being married takes them further away from God. That conclusion is, of course, ridiculous, opposed to the teaching of Eph. 5:21–3 and *Gaudium et Spes* 48, which I discussed above, as well as being a contradiction of our own experience of life, where the chaste and fruitful love of dedicated and loyal married couples has been one of the most wonderful places of God's revelation among men and women of all ages. A careful analysis of the biblical material provides a different answer.

## Contemporary Biblical Criticism of Matt. 19:12 and 1 Cor. 7:32–5

I mentioned above that there is some doubt among biblical scholars as to whether it is correct to use these passages as the biblical background for the vow of chastity. I wish to approach this biblical material in two steps. First I wish to show how contemporary exegesis questions the traditional use of the texts, and secondly I would like to see if it is possible, after all, to find a more positive theology of chastity *from the same texts*.

### Matthew 19:12

As in all literary criticism, this famous passage on being a 'eunuch' must not be pulled out of its context and ex-

plained as if it was the only thing which Matthew reported
from Jesus. It has a place in a whole Gospel, and within
its own immediate context. It is precisely from the study
of Matt. 19:12 within its context that scholars have come
to doubt whether it is correctly used to speak of celibacy.

It comes as the final 'punch line' in the passage which
runs from Matt. 19:3–12. The first part of the passage is
taken up with a discussion between Jesus and the Pharisees
(vv. 3–9). This passage is paralleled by Mark 10:1–12. The
second part of the passage (vv. 10–12) is made up of a
discussion with the disciples, and has no parallel in the
rest of the New Testament. This should already put us on
our guard. Matt. 19:10–12 is a passage which Matthew
has added to his source, Mark 10:2–9, so he wants to say
something special with this addition.

The encounter with the Pharisees follows the form of
a Rabbinic discussion. In the first century there was a
discussion over the causes of divorce. There were two
schools of thought. A Rabbi Shammai insisted (interpreting Deut. 24:1) that one could only divorce one's wife
when there was a serious cause, while Rabbi Hillel (interpreting the same text) said that a divorce was possible for
any reason at all. In Matt. 19:3, Jesus' opinion is sought
on this matter, as they ask him: 'Is it lawful to divorce
one's wife *for any cause*', obviously wanting to see if he
agreed with Hillel's position. Jesus' answer follows a good
Rabbinic practice, as he quotes from the Law of Moses
(Gen. 1:27 and 2:24), but he interprets these texts in a way
which cuts across the question of divorce by saying that
it is impossible: 'What therefore God has joined together,
let not man put asunder' (Matt. 19:4–6). The Pharisees,
not to be beaten, also go to the Law of Moses (Deut. 24:1)
and ask why a bill of divorce was allowed by Moses
himself, if there was to be no divorce (v. 7). Jesus tells
them that it was because of the hardness of the heart of
Israel that this happened, and then abandoning all refer-

ence to the Law of Moses he announces: 'And I say to
you: whoever divorces his wife, except for unchastity,
and marries another, commits adultery' (v. 9). Jesus lays
down a prohibition of divorce, allowing only one exception. It is important to notice that Mark 10:11, which
Matthew is using here, does not have 'except for unchastity'. In fact, the rest of the New Testament (see 1 Cor.
7:10–11; Luke 16:18; Mark 10:2–12) is absolute in its prohibition of divorce. Only Matthew, therefore, has added
this exception, just as he has added vv. 10–12. We must
ask why Matthew added these passages, but we must first
take our analysis further.

We are now in the passage (vv. 10–12) which is found
only in Matthew. The disciples are stunned by the severity
of Jesus' teaching and they exclaim: 'If such is the case of
a man with his wife, it is not expedient to marry' (v. 10).
Translated into modern terms, the disciples are saying: 'If
I cannot get rid of her, I would be better off if I did not
marry her in the first place!' Jesus' answer to this (v. 11)
is to point out that it is no longer 'the case of a man with
his wife'. What he had just announced is an entirely new
situation which cannot be measured by merely human and
social criteria. He is talking about the wonderful gift
which is called *Christian* marriage: 'Not all men can receive
this precept, but only those to whom it is given' (v. 11).
We are no longer dealing simply with the human, social
and sexual situation of a man with a woman, but the
'graced' situation, the gift of Christian marriage. It is its
specifically Christian character which makes it indissolu-
ble. We then come to v. 12: 'For there are eunuchs who
have been so from birth, and there are eunuchs who have
been made eunuchs by men, and there are eunuchs who
have made themselves eunuchs for the sake of the Kingdom of heaven. He who is able to receive this, let him
receive it.'

What are we to make of this passage in a context which

is *entirely* made up of a discussion of divorce? If the passage is about consecrated celibacy, how does it relate to the rest of the context? This problem has led scholars to seek different solutions, but we must go back to the fact that Matthew, who is largely following Mark 10:2–12, has added two important further passages: 'except for un-chastity' in v. 9 and the passage leading to and including the eunuch saying in vv. 11–12. If Matthew has added these passages, then we must suppose that he has done so for a purpose. There must have been some urgent pastoral concern in the community for which he wrote his Gospel that he was trying to assist by these additions.

It is nowadays generally admitted that the Gospel of Matthew was written for a community largely composed of Jewish Christians facing difficulties on two fronts:

1. The expulsion from the ancient Torah-centred life-style when official Judaism gradually came to see that any sect which believed that Jesus was 'the Christ' could not re-main in its ranks.
2. The Christian message, largely couched in Jewish terms and dependent upon Jewish tradition, was now being preached to the Gentiles, and they were joining the community without any Jewish background.

It seems that Matthew had to face two serious problems in questions of Christian marriage among those Gentiles who came into the community without any Jewish back-ground or formation. In the first place, there were some who were married in a way which Jewish law (Lev. 18:6–18) regarded as incestuous. We have a clear indication that this was happening from Paul's discussion of it in 1 Cor. 5:1–5. Exactly the same expression which Matthew uses to speak of 'unchastity' in v. 9 (Greek: *porneia*) is used by Paul to speak of the incestuous situation in Corinth (1 Cor. 5:1). This is the situation where Matthew allows divorce. There is to be no divorce, except for these cases

of incestuous relationships between people who had come
to the Christian community from a culture where that
same relationship was perfectly normal. But this was not
the only problem that the ex-pagan converts seemed to be
causing for the community. Some would have come into
the community, married there, but then, at a later stage,
disenchanted, left, returning to their former culture and
religion to marry and live on outside the Christian community. The problem to be faced here was that one partner
of the marriage would have remained in the Christian
community, still linked to his or her former partner by
the bond of Christian marriage. How does Matthew solve
this problem? He takes a very hard line and asks them to
remain unmarried, to become 'eunuchs for the sake of the
kingdom of heaven' (19:12). Matthew was well aware that
what he was asking was extremely difficult, in fact, impossible, were it not for the grace of God. Therefore he
adds, 'He who is able to receive this, let him receive it',
and then, a little later in the same context, the words of
encouragement: 'With men this is impossible, but with
God all things are possible' (19:26).

It appears to me that this is the best explanation of Matt.
19:12 because it solves three problems which 19:3–12 has
always presented to interpreters:
1. To explain why Matthew inserted his exception clause
to 19:9 and the passage from vv. 10–12.
2. What is more important is that it explains *both* inser-
tions by relating them to the *same* pastoral problem: the
difficulties faced by the irregular marital situation of the
converted ex-pagans.
3. It explains v. 12 within the context of vv. 3–12. It is
not left hanging limply on to the end of the passage as
some sort of strange unconnected saying about consecrated celibacy.

The problem with this explanation, however, is that the
traditional use of Matt. 19:12 can no longer be made. We

must note carefully what we have seen so far. Up to this point I have examined what *Matthew* is saying in Matt. 19:3–12. I pointed out that vv. 3–9 come from Mark 10:2–12, but where did Matthew find v. 12? Did he invent it? There are very good reasons which indicate that he did not, but we will return to that after a consideration of 1 Cor. 7:32–5.

## 1 Corinthians 7:32–5

A reading of this passage seems to show clearly that Paul advocates the state of celibacy as a superior state for a Christian:

> I want you to be free from anxieties. The unmarried man is anxious about the affairs of the Lord, how to please the Lord; but the married man is anxious about worldly affairs, how to please his wife, and his interests are divided. And the unmarried woman or girl is anxious about the affairs of the Lord, how to be holy in body and spirit; but the married woman is anxious about worldly affairs, how to please her husband. I say this for your own benefit, not to lay any restraint upon you, but to promote good order and to secure your undivided devotion to the Lord.

Once again, however, we must situate the passage in its context. In the passage which immediately precedes 7:32–5, Paul speaks about a series of worldly and human activities which must become relative.

> I think that *in view of the present distress* it is well for a person to remain as he is . . . I mean, brethren, that *the appointed time has grown very short*; from now on let those who have wives live as though they had none, and those who mourn as though they were not mourning, and those who rejoice as though they were not rejoicing

. . . *For the form of this world is passing away.* (7:26, 29–30, 31).

In this passage Paul gives his reasons why he believes that people must drop all attention to ordinary affairs:
in view of the present distress
the appointed time has grown very short
the form of this world is passing away.

What does Paul mean by these expressions? It is clear that the early Paul was convinced and urged on in his preaching because he believed that the final end time, the return of the Lord, was only just around the corner. It is evident from his very first letters, the letters to the Thessalonians (written in the late 40s), that he had preached this message of the imminent return of the Lord with such conviction that the Christians had decided that all they had to do was sit and wait. There was no longer any need to apply themselves to their day-to-day tasks, if the Day of the Lord was about to arrive (see 1 Thess. 4:13—5:11 and the whole of 2 Thessalonians). The first letter to the Corinthians was probably written shortly after, in A.D. 54. Paul is still finding the urgency of his message in the conviction that all is about to end very shortly. It is because of this conviction that he can so strongly advocate that his Corinthian community devote all their time and attention, not to wives, husbands, mourning, rejoicing, buying, selling and dealing with the world (see 1 Cor. 7:29–31) but so that they might secure their undivided attention and devotion to the Lord who was about to come (see 7:35).

But he did not come – and he still has not come. If Paul's teaching on celibacy is so intimately linked to his presupposition that the end time is at hand, does this teaching not become somewhat relative when the end time does not come? In fact, Paul's own understanding of the end time develops. He was able to see, as the years passed by, that the Church was going to face a long history and thus several of the positions he takes in later letters vary from those found in the Thessalonian correspondence and 1 Corinthians. If the end time is near at hand, there is no need for a theology of marriage, but if the Church is going to work its way through history, then such a theology is urgently needed – and it was the Pauline point of view in Eph. 5:21–3, that was used in *Gaudium et Spes* 48.

Having said all this, however, a word of warning must be issued. We must not rule out the central point of Paul's teaching. Notice that he states his purpose in 1 Cor. 7:32 – 'I want you to be free from anxieties.' Anything which stands between the Christian and his total adhesion to the Lord must be regarded as secondary. One of these things can be the problems which arise from the care and love of a spouse. Paul is not *primarily* concerned about celibacy or marriage; he is concerned that his Christians be one in joy, love and hope, freed from any anxieties which may destroy such central factors in the 'life in Christ'. The only thing that matters for Paul is that his Christians are consumed by an 'undivided devotion to the Lord'. As we shall see shortly, here Paul is close to Jesus' own understanding of the function of a celibate life.

Nevertheless, we again find that a study of the whole context of the passage, used by the traditional argument to exalt the celibate state in the Church, rather lessens its significance. Are we, then, without biblical support for this state of life within the Church? Has it come about because of some strange mentality in the early years of the Church, a lack of appreciation of the value of creation and human love as places where a God of love can be authentically revealed? I think not. Here we must return to our consideration of Matt. 19:12.

## The Eunuch Saying on the Lips of Jesus

As I concluded my treatment of what the eunuch passage meant *within the context of Matt. 19:3–12*, I asked the question: Where did Matthew find v. 12? Did he invent it or did it come to him from some source? It is widely accepted that Matthew did *not* invent 19:12, but that he found it among the remembered words of Jesus himself. Scholars have various criteria for determining whether or not certain passages were composed in the early Church, or whether they come from Jesus himself. The following are the main reasons which force us to conclude that Matt. 19:12 is something that Jesus actually said:

1. The word 'eunuch' is a very harsh expression. It is a bad enough word today, but in the first century, when these men were actually a rejected part of society, it was offensive and crude. There is no way that the early Church would have invented a saying which spoke of Jesus or his followers in such terms. If it is found in the Gospel, then it must have been said by Jesus. Despite the continual use of this very crude word, Matthew includes the passage because Jesus himself had said it.

2. The structure of the passage is typical of a semitic proverbial type passage, where the listener (or reader) is gradually led through a rhythmic play on a word, to the final point at the end of the passage. This form is clear even in the English Translation: 'There are eunuchs . . . and there are eunuchs . . . who have been made eunuchs . . . and there are eunuchs . . . who have made themselves eunuchs.' This means that it comes from an Aramaic-speaking background.

3. Although Luke and Mark (understandably) do not report this passage, it does turn up *in a slightly different form* in Justin Martyr and Epiphanius, two early Fathers of the Church. This suggests that they had also heard or seen this passage, but in a form slightly different from Matt.

19:12. They probably had it from an independent source, so Matthew did not invent it.

The most important factor, however, lies in the impossibility of seeing a situation in the life of the early Church which would have caused them to invent this passage. It must be there because Jesus said it and if Jesus said it, we must try and discover why he said it and what it meant to him. The attitude of people in first-century Judaism towards eunuchs was extremely negative, yet the 'eunuch' theme is central to Matt. 19:12. Despite its crudeness and its offensive implications it is used in a noun and in a verbal form, no less than five times in this one verse. Why would Jesus use such an expression?

There is ample evidence in the Gospels that Jesus was the object of continual abuse from his opponents. He and his disciples do not fast (Mark 2:18), they violate the Sabbath (Mark 2:23) and they take their meals without the ritual lustrations (Mark 7:5). Jesus himself is called 'a glutton and a drunkard, a friend of tax collectors and sinners' (Matt. 11:19). 'You are a Samaritan and have a demon,' accuse the Jews in John 8:48, and on another occasion we are told that 'they have called the master of the household Beelzebub' (Matt. 10:25). It appears that this process of heaping abuse on Jesus was a normal way of attack, and it seems more than probable that another term used to attack Jesus was 'Eunuch!' Given the importance of marriage and the procreation of children, in obedience to Gen. 1:28, it appears more than probable that there was something about the life-style of Jesus of Nazareth which gave his opponents the chance to call him 'Eunuch!' in a derogatory and abusive sense. Matt. 19:12 on the lips of Jesus was his calm reply to the attacks from his enemies who sought any excuse to hurl abuse at this troublesome character. Jesus was a celibate and was thus immediately open to such abuse, particularly as he was a public figure who troubled the establishment by the quality and authority of his life and preaching. I would suggest that one of the reasons why this particular 'word of Jesus' remained alive in the tradition, despite the harshness of the word 'eunuch' was because it was Jesus' regular answer to a regular form of abuse which was aimed at him. Readers will be well aware that this form of abuse has not died out over the centuries. When all forms of logical and rational argument can no longer win the day, all languages and cultures with which I am familiar turn readily to a form of abuse which attacks a man's sexual capacities. My own Australian 'popular culture' is extremely rich in such expressions!

It is not enough to establish, through our modern critical methods, the fact that a celibate Jesus replied to his enemies in the terms of Matt. 19:12. What is most important for us is to ask just what the saying meant for Jesus. Now we are right back into the heart of the subject of this chapter. We are now touching the reason why Jesus lived his life of chastity as a celibate. In Matt. 19:12 Matthew's context seems to be addressed to ex-pagan Christians who now find themselves alone and cannot remarry, but the passage had its origins on the *lips of Jesus*, and there it meant something quite different: why Jesus was celibate.

It has been traditional to understand the reason for being a eunuch as 'for the sake of the Kingdom of Heaven' in a final sense. This means that one is celibate so that one may be free and able to give oneself for the construction of the Kingdom of Heaven. This is the way *Perfectae Caritatis* 12 uses Matt. 19:12 and this is the source of my major difficulty with the passage from the Council. The original Greek text means more than that. The Greek uses a preposition (*dia* + accusative case) which indicates that Jesus announced that he was celibate 'because of' the Kingdom of Heaven. He was not a celibate 'so that' he might construct the Kingdom, but 'because of ' the overwhelming presence of the Kingdom. The Greek indicates that this is the primary meaning of the passage. It is the overwhelming power of the presence of the Kingdom in his life that led Jesus to celibacy. We must now explain Matt. 19:12 in this light. Jesus' opponents knew of two types of eunuch: the one born so and the one made so by man. Like Jesus, these people were 'unable' to accept a normal married situation. However, the motive for Jesus' inability was not physical. He was so taken over by the urgent presence of the Kingdom that he could do no other than give himself entirely to it. The celibacy of Jesus was not something which he made happen to himself by first deliberating whether or not it should happen, and then deciding in favour of it so that he would be free to dedicate himself entirely to the construction of the Kingdom to come. The causality ran in the opposite direction. In Jesus of Nazareth the guiding principle and the overwhelming experience of his life was the presence of the lordship of God whom he called 'Father' (see Matt. 11:27; Mark 13:32; 14:36; Luke 11:2 and the whole of the Fourth Gospel). It was this 'lordship' which led him to his state of celibacy, to his being a eunuch *because of* the overwhelming presence of the Kingdom in his life, and suddenly 1 Cor. 7:32–5 regains its sense.

We saw in our consideration of that passage that Paul claimed that marriage (and many other ordinary occupations) became relative in the light of the imminent return of the Lord. We also saw, however, that contemporary exegesis tends to take the sting out of Paul's claims as he was not correct in his ideas about the immediate return of the Lord. However, a celibacy lived under the urgent presence of the Kingdom of God again makes sense of Paul's argument. As we saw in our analysis of 1 Cor. 7:32–5, what ultimately concerned Paul was the establishment of a community where all that mattered was 'life in Christ', the joy, hope, love and unity which can be created by an 'undivided devotion to the Lord'. While contemporary exegesis is correct in claiming that we must not make this an important New Testament teaching on the relative value of marriage, Paul, like Jesus, lived under the divine urgency of the overpowering presence of the Kingdom. Paul may have been mistaken about the immediate return of the Lord, but he is surely correct when he insists that all that matters is our 'life in Christ'. As this is the case, there is no need to wait for the end time; the eschatological moment is *now*, because the Lord has taken me over *now*. To apply the words of Paul to the experience of Jesus, we can say that he lived a chaste celibacy because of an undivided attention to his Lord, God whom he called Father (see 1 Cor. 7:35).

## The Function of the Vow of Chastity Today

Thus far I have been speaking about how Jesus saw and spoke about *his* celibacy. However, his reply to his opponents is not just a defence of himself and an explanation of why he was not married. It would have been then, and still remains today, an invitation to all those who hear this quiet reply to strident abuse to consider just what the Kingdom might hold if it has so determined the life of Jesus. Here is the authentically and radically evangelical basis for a life of celibacy. No longer are our lives based on an odd text which somehow was tacked on to the end of a discussion of divorce, but they are rooted in the life-style of Jesus himself.

Like Jesus, we are chaste because of the overwhelming presence of God's Kingdom which keeps crowding in on us. In other words, our ongoing decision for chastity is intelligible as a decision which comes about within the context of a major religious experience, just as the decision for marriage comes about within the context of a major religious experience. The term 'religious experience' is a technical term. It does not refer to experiences which 'religious' people have. They are experiences which are somehow beyond our control. They are greater than us: love, tears, hope, anguish, joy and laughter. No matter what we believe, it is a part of the experience of every man and woman. Why does this particular man marry that particular girl? So many other combinations would have been possible, but something unique has happened between these two people. In an authentic situation, they 'fall in love'. The English expression is good as it is a genuine 'falling', out of human control and measurement. They can do no other. There is a kingdom established between the two of them that renders them existentially incapable of doing anything else. All of this happens *before* any decision to marry. So must it be with the decision for chastity. A life of chastity is nothing else but the existential consequence which flows out of the prior experience of the urgent presence of the Kingdom of God. This is what it means to be 'a eunuch for the sake of the kingdom of heaven' (Matt. 19:12), drawn into a situation where all that matters is that we be 'anxious about the affairs of the Lord' (see 1 Cor. 7:32–5).

A very important consequence of this re-reading of our traditional texts is that it gives the celibate every right to his place in society alongside all classes of men and women, married and unmarried. No longer can the celibate be regarded as deprived, deformed or in some way 'strange'. No longer is the life of chastity a 'stiff-upper-lip' and a 'gritting your teeth' business. Where we stand as celibates flows out of exactly the same sort of experience which led that man to marry that woman: the overpowering presence of a Kingdom of love. Just as, in an authentic situation of sexual love, they can do no other than marry and consecrate themselves to each other and their families, so also the celibate, in an authentic situation of celibate love, can do no other than be a eunuch because of the

Kingdom of love in his life. Seen in this *parallel* fashion, instead of the all-too-familiar *contrasting* fashion, these two different ways of living out the same overpowering experience can be mutually enriched. The celibate learns from married couples that God's love is revealed through the affective life of his creatures, while the married can see from the life of the celibate that the source of this love ultimately transcends what their limited human affection can ever hope to demonstrate.

All Christians are called to a chaste love, because this is the only sort of love which creates. The exhilarating and joyful *total* gift of self can take place only in the context of a profound loyalty and trust. The Scriptures parallel it with the gift of Christ for the Church and the Church says of it that it is 'caught up into divine love and is directed and enriched by the redemptive power of Christ and the salvific action of the Church' (*Gaudium et Spes* 48). Why is this so? What is so special about this 'gift' of authentic married love? It is the unique place among men and women where the affective nature of a God who is love is revealed to the world. The Gospels tell us that God loved so much that the Incarnation had to burst forth from the immensity of that love (see John 3:16). Love is not love unless it is felt – and this is the love which is revealed by authentic married love – the call to chastity of the major part of Christianity.

Need I list the signs of the times? – the use of sex to sell all sorts of innocent wares, and to add spice to an already drugged society; the education of the young to a life-style where to give and receive oneself totally is like sharing a cup of coffee – as long as both parties think it may be a useful experience; the breakdown of marriage and the family. It is pointless to go on, as we all live – and often wonder at ourselves – in the context of this new dogma of 'If you like it, do it!'

Religious, vowed to their particular form of chastity,

are not superior in this department. The pain which a chaste life can often cause tells us that. However, we are calling out to a topsy-turvy world that they may have abundant pleasure, but they have lost love. Swept off our feet by the Lordship of a God who is love, we show the world that genuine affection is not found in a predatory man or woman hunt, but in the loss of self, as we are taken over by the presence of so great a love that we can do no other than give ourselves uniquely to this love. As I have already said, this does not make it any easier, but from here we can speak to all Christians; we can announce, through the joy of a free and unconditional love that the exquisite experience of loving and belonging to the loved one is not something which we can determine, but is a reflection of the loving gift of a caring, creating, fruitful and loving God: 'But God shows his love for us in that while we were yet sinners, Christ died for us' (Rom. 5:8). Again, the function of our chaste love is not to make us something different or 'odd' within the context of the universal call to sanctity, but to call all Christians back to the authentic, faithful, loving and joyful gift of self which is the mark of all Christians, celibate or married.

## Conclusions

Behind this re-interpretation of our traditional biblical background for a life of chastity stands the conviction that our celibate lives have their source and strength from our stance *vis-à-vis* a God of love. If they do, then we will not be afraid to take the risk of loving. Chaste celibate love all too often leads to a spineless 'being nice' to everyone, causing us to shy clear of the cut and thrust of the challenge of a genuine closeness to other people. This was not the way of Jesus of Nazareth, and it must not be the way of those people who follow him. Within the context of our Religious life our being taken over by this Kingdom of love must be reflected in and witnessed to the world by the *quality of our love*, that is, the *quality of our life together*: our community life. We are not *primarily* chaste so that we will be free to work, even though *Perfectae Caritatis* indicates that this is one of the major functions of a vow of chastity. Jerome Murphy-O'Connor stated the case well when he wrote:

> It is an unfortunate paradox, but the idea that celibacy frees for universal love is one of the major reasons why religious communities have failed to fulfill their witness potential, because inevitably this gives rise to the view that the community is merely a base *from which* the real work is done. The result is that religious communities become loveless deserts. Not only does this make celibacy virtually impossible because man cannot live without love, but it means that the outsider who is shocked into asking 'What makes them different?' finds nothing but a verbal answer to his question. The real answer, the existential answer, is lacking. Not unnaturally, then, celibate life is judged to be meaningless. (*What is Religious Life?* p. 59)

Again, when we come to examine our consciences about the significance of our chaste lives, we must start 'at home'.

A difficulty in living the life of chastity is often at the basis of both community and individual crises. I know that what follows is frequently said, but it bears repeating. All sorts of lack of love and sinfulness – back-biting conversations, deep divisions among confreres, carelessness about prayer and a lazy living off the hard work of the rest of the community – are tolerated. A difficulty in the affective area, however, all too often leads to a rapid decision that the person in question is 'out of place'. It is often difficult to find, in this situation, the same tolerance, love and understanding that are given to other problems.

Yet, as far as the New Testament is concerned, discussions of moral questions centre their attention on the basic law of Christianity: the law of love. Among us, however, failures against the community, poverty and obedience are tolerated, but often the stern defence of the aspect of our lives which should show the quality of our love, serves only to demonstrate its absence. In the Gospels, as far as affective problems are concerned, the sinners in question receive no condemnation, but pardon (see, for example, John 8:1–11). Of course, it is not always the community which is at fault. Very often in these difficult situations, many would like to reach out a loving, forgiving and caring hand and heart to the person in difficulty, but the offer is refused. Behind a great deal of this tendency stands the limitation of this vow to the physical state of being a celibate. When physical difficulties arise, people panic, forgetting that no matter how sinful they may be, a God of love forgives and calls them back to their commitment to chastity.

In the light of this, we must learn to be patient with these difficulties, both our own and those of others. It is precisely here that the love and support of the people with whom we live are absolutely vital. Rollo May, the celebrated psychologist, has spoken of the sure sign of a mature and integrated personality as being 'the courage of imperfection'. We must allow ourselves the exhilaration, genuinely felt, and shown, and not just spoken about, which comes from loving and being loved. Only in this way and through this *experience* can we come closer to understanding a God who is defined as love (1 John 4:8 and 16). Only then will we be able to see why we can and must be so swept off our feet by the urgent presence of the Lordship of that God.

The celibate must not be seen, either by himself or by others, as outside the experience of genuine human affection. The question of close friendships among celibates arises. There is a growing recognition of this phenomenon within the Religious life and some pastoral and theological research and reflection are now being devoted to it. It is timely, but a knowledge of the history of the Religious life indicates that it is not a new phenomenon. It appears to me that there are four basic principles which should govern such relationships.

1. They must not be condemned out of hand. The fear of 'particular friendships' should be a thing of the past, although difficulties, mistakes and even sinfulness can occur here, as in all aspects of our lives.
2. These friendships must never be sought out; they must arise and happen in a context of mutually shared prayer, work and ideals. A Religious *looking for* a friend will soon find one, usually with painful consequences.
3. Directly related to the point just made, Religious should *never* establish close affective bonds with non-celibates. Although these relationships almost always begin full of hope and good will, the non-celibate partner understandably will eventually (however subtly) make demands which the celibate cannot hope to fulfil.
4. The people in the relationship should be directed by people *outside* the relationship. Again, experience teaches us that self-direction leads to self-deception.

These principles may sound simple enough, but they are very difficult to live out in full. It is only possible among people who have their priorities right. Their primary commitment must be the 'life in Christ' which they have in and through their immediate community and their particular Religious family; their finding of the God who inspires them to love in a deep, long and patient prayer life. Even when all this is a part of their lives the cross will loom large, if their friendship is genuine, because there must always be a readiness to 'let go'. In this situation, the words of the Psalmist always come to my mind:

'Because he cleaves to me in love, I will free him' (Ps. 91:14, A.T.). It is especially here (but not only here) that one can see the value of the early Church's association of martyrdom theology with virginity. Many Religious are unable to cope with this pain, and relationships run into difficulty, as one or other of the parties tries to possess rather than free the other. As married people would be quick to tell us, here we show our affective immaturity. The married also must be able to 'let go'. It is one of the most important aspects of a successful and mature conjugal relationship. This is always painful, but it is a pain which frees for authentic love.

Although he was writing in quite another context. William H. Vanstone has written a passage which applies beautifully to this aspect of genuine celibate love:

> Among the circumstances which restrict the expression of love is the capacity of the other to receive. A parent knows the danger of overwhelming or imprisoning a child by expressions of love which are untimely or excessive. A friend knows that expressions of friendship too sudden or demonstrative may simply embarrass. A wife knows that, out of love for her husband, she must sometimes 'think about herself'. The external restraint which love practises is often a mark of its freedom from internal limit. Love does not lay down the condition that it must be allowed freedom to express itself, nor limit its activity to those circumstances in which it may freely act. Love accepts without limit the discipline of circumstances. Although it always aspires to enlarge its own activity, it sometimes finds its most generous enlargement in the acceptance of restraint. Love must sometimes express itself in the renunciation of not disclosing itself. (*Love's Endeavour, Love's Expense. The Response of Being to the Love of God*, p. 44)

In recent years many close celibate friends have wondered

about the ultimate significance of the experience of love which has come into their celibate lives. Vanstone gives us the answer: 'The external restraint which love practises is often a mark of its freedom from internal limit'. It must be so, because a celibacy caused by the overpowering experience of the Kingdom of a God of love knows no internal limit.

All of us are made for intimacy. We must face this squarely, convinced that to live properly Christian lives is to live whole lives. Men and women usually resolve the crisis of intimacy when they choose one another. From that moment on all other options are existentially impossible because of the 'Kingdom' which has been established between them. So must the celibate also spend his or her life resolving the crisis of intimacy 'because of the Kingdom', and then it may be said at Vatican III of the lives of celibates, what Vatican II said about married love: 'Authentic [celibate] love is caught up into divine love and is directed and enriched by the redemptive power of Christ and the salvific action of the Church' (see *Gaudium et Spes* 48).

# OBEDIENCE

As I introduced the question of chastity, I argued against the tendency to single out the vow of celibate chastity as the distinguishing mark of the Religious, and I suggested that we maintain the traditional terms and order for the vows: poverty, chastity and obedience. However, there can be little doubt that the Gospel imperative which encompasses all Gospel values is obedience. In fact, there are ancient traditions of the Religious life in the Church where the only vow taken is obedience, as the rest is seen to follow logically from it. Because this is the case, it is also the most radically demanding of all the imperatives, and the reader may be somewhat overwhelmed by the idealistic nature of what I am about to propose. Indeed, I am sensitive to the idealism of all that I have written so far. There is a huge gap between the reality of the consecrated life which we are attempting to live as individuals and in community, and the ideals which I am presenting here. Nevertheless, we must not hesitate in our attempts, in the light of the Word of God, to find the ideal model against which, and in the light of which, we should continually examine our commitment to 'the following of Christ as it is put before us in the Gospel' (*Perfectae Caritatis* 2). Precisely because these reflections are biblical reflections they are idealistic, but the scriptures never apologize for their idealism. St Paul does not say: 'Love *should be* patient

and kind; love *should not be* jealous or boastful'. He says:
'Love *is* patient and kind; love *is not* jealous or boastful'
(1 Cor. 13:4). I am also attempting to avoid the condi-
tional, and to present the biblical model as an imperative,
idealistic though that imperative might be. As we turn
now to examine the biblical model for Christian obedience
and authority, this aspect of the Christian vocation might
appear to be an almost impossible dream. Despite this
fact, we must face the radical nature of the ideal to which
we have been called, to which we have responded in
baptism, and to which we daily commit ourselves in our
ongoing decision to live in a Christian community.

Despite the insistence of a long tradition in the Religious
life, and my own indications above, that obedience encompasses all the Gospel values, it is surprising to find
that there is no single text from the New Testament which
has provided a consistent biblical background to the vow
and practice of obedience. We have already seen that discussions of poverty centred their attention on the Jerusalem community, as it is reported in the early chapters of
the Acts of the Apostles, the Beatitudes and the story of
the rich young man. Chaste celibacy, it has been long
argued, is based upon the eunuch saying in Matt. 19:12,
and Paul's advice to the Corinthian Church that they
would do well to remain unmarried, so that they could
devote all their energies and attention to the Lord seemed
to show the superiority of the celibate state. None of these
so-called 'proof-texts' are available for an immediate solution to the question of obedience. Yet, more than any of
the vows, this is the one which is most biblical. This is
the case because behind the call to obedience in the Christian life stands the call to follow the life-style of Jesus of
Nazareth. We have already indicated that Jesus was poor,
and that Jesus was chaste, but both of these aspects of his
life pale into insignificance before the grandeur of his

obedience. His life was dominated by a profound openness to God, whom he called his Father.

## The Obedience of Jesus

I cannot hope to do justice to this question within a few short pages. I merely wish to give some general indications of the centrality of obedience for a correct understanding of Jesus of Nazareth.

### What did Jesus think he was doing?

There is a very short answer to this important question, as scholars are in universal agreement that Jesus of Nazareth saw his mission as the establishment of the Kingdom of God among men. In Mark's Gospel, Jesus bursts upon the scene announcing, 'The time is fulfilled and the Kingdom of God is at hand; repent and believe in the Gospel' (Mark 1:15). Our English expression 'the Kingdom of God', however, does not do justice to the notion which seemed to dominate the preaching of Jesus, as the word 'kingdom' is a rather static concept. It smacks of a territory with borders within which a certain king has authority. There are no such limits to the kingdom which Jesus was preaching, and many scholars suggest, helpfully, that we would do better to speak of Jesus' announcing the Reign of God, with its more dynamic idea of the active presence of God as king.

How can scholars be so certain that the preaching of the inbreak of the active reign of God in the hearts and lives of men and women stood at the centre of Jesus' preaching? This certainly arises out of the centrality of the notion of the Reign of God in Jesus' parables. Of all the material in the Gospels, we are in contact with the powerful yet simple preaching of Jesus of Nazareth in the parables. They were short and pungent, and they were imprinted indelibly in the minds and hearts of the first listeners to

Jesus' own preaching. They were then faithfully passed on
down through a generation, until they came to be record-
ed in the Gospels. Each Evangelist, of course, uses them
in his own way, and Matthew, a careful Jewish scholar,
even avoids the sacred name 'God' and speaks of 'the
Kingdom of Heaven', but his faithfulness to the original
preaching of Jesus holds firm. There is a parable to touch
upon every aspect of the Reign of God among men:

> The kingdom of God is as if a man should scatter seed
> upon the ground (Mark 4:26);
> With what can we compare the kingdom of God? . . .
> It is like a grain of mustard seed (Mark 4:30);
> The kingdom of heaven may be compared to a man
> who sowed good seed in his field (Matt. 13:24);
> The kingdom of heaven is like leaven which a woman
> took and hid in three measures of meal, till it was all
> leavened (Matt. 13:33);
> The kingdom of heaven is like a net which was thrown
> into the sea and gathered fish of every kind (Matt.
> 13:47).

The list could go on, as I have merely used some passages
from two famous collections of parable material in Mark
4 and Matt. 13. We cannot delay here to discuss the nature
of the Kingdom, but it should be clear that one of the
unique things about Jesus of Nazareth was his burning
conviction that the active Reign of God had broken into
the world, the hearts, the minds and the lives of men and
women in his person, his activity – especially his miracu-
lous activity (see Luke 11:20: 'If it is by the finger of God
that I cast out demons, then the kingdom of God has
come upon you'), and his preaching. The Reign of God
was already present, but not yet fulfilled; it brought peace,
joy, harmony, but also challenges and responsibilities; it
grew silently and swiftly, and was to be treasured beyond
all treasures. Above all, it could not be dismissed in its

power to transform men and women. If this is what Jesus claimed to have brought, then the question which must be asked, and all too rapidly answered, is the question that his contemporaries were all asking: 'Who does this man think he is?' (see, for example, Mark 1:27; 2:7; 4:41; 6:2; John 12:34). According to the Gospels, he understood himself as a Son and as the Son of Man.

## Jesus as a Son

We must be careful in our approach to this aspect of the historical Jesus, as perhaps the central christological belief of the Christian Church, despite a small group of vocal Christian dissenters, is that Jesus of Nazareth was the Son of God. There can be little doubt that even the earliest of the Gospels, Mark, confesses this belief (see Mark 1:1; 1:11; 9:7; 15:39) and it grows in the Gospel tradition until it becomes the christological category which dominates the Fourth Gospel. There are too many passages to list, but it should be sufficient merely to recall the Fourth Evangelist's confession of his purpose for writing his Gospel: 'These things are written that you may go on believing that Jesus is the Christ, the Son of God, and that believing you may have life in his name' (John 20:31 A.T.). However, all of this is post-resurrectional, rendering *explicit* in the Spirit-filled confessing Church what was *implicit* in the life and experience of the historical Jesus. What was Jesus' own attitude to his sonship?

Here we are at the centre of an enormous discussion among specialists. It appears to me that the answer is simple enough. There can be little doubt that Jesus of Nazareth was aware of some sort of unique relationship with the God of Israel. For a pious Jew, Jahweh was their very own powerful God, but such reverence had to be given to this God that they dare not even pronounce his name. We have just seen how Matthew, a Jewish author, still respects this when he changes 'the Kingdom of God'

into the circumlocution 'the Kingdom of Heaven'. Indeed,
there are places in Jewish literature where Jewish authors
speak of Israel as 'a son of God', in so far as she was a
faithful and obedient observer of his laws. She had even
developed an idea of a Messiah who would be a 'son of
God' from centuries of reflection on two biblical passages
which promised that God would raise up a son (2 Sam.
7:14 and Ps. 2:7). Jesus, however, spoke to the God of
Israel in terms of 'Abba'. In Mark 14:36 he uses the term
explicitly: 'Abba, Father, all things are possible to thee;
remove this cup from me; yet not what I will, but what
thou wilt.' Here we have the perfect paradigm of Jesus'
approach to the God of Israel, whom he called 'Abba',
Father, and to whom he was always and everywhere
obedient. It is important to understand that the term 'Abba' could only be used within an actual obedient and
loving Father–Son relationship. Modern Hebrew still has
it. A young child running down the street to meet his
father would call out 'Abba', and any other use of it would
be senseless. Never before had anyone dared to speak to
the God of Israel in such endearing and close terms. It
appears that this was a regular form of prayer for Jesus.
Although it does not appear again in the Gospels, there
are many places where Jesus speaks to God directly as
'Father' (Greek: *pater*), and most scholars would admit
that here the Evangelists were translating into Greek what
was originally the endearing and extremely personal Ar-
amaic word 'Abba'.

This evidence points to a very important consideration
about Jesus' understanding of himself. He clearly saw himself as related to the God of Israel in terms of an obedient
son. This throws further light on the urgency behind the
life of Jesus which can be found behind all the Gospels; an
urgency to go on into a future into which, he believed,
God his Father was leading him. All he could do was
respond radically, without ever swerving from the will

and plan of God, his Father. What this meant will be seen in my brief consideration of Jesus as the Son of Man, but there is one further aspect of the Sonship of Jesus which must be mentioned. The historical Jesus lived out a life of sonship in terms of a complete and radical obedience, cost what it may. This is what the Letter to the Hebrews is referring to when the author writes:

> In the days of his flesh, Jesus offered up prayers and supplications, with loud cries and tears, to him who was able to save him from death, and he was heard for his godly fear. Although he was a Son, he learned obedience through suffering. (Heb. 5:7–8)

But it did not stop there. There is a passage, common to Matthew and Luke, and thus more ancient than both of them, which comes like a bolt from the sky in the synoptic tradition, announcing that this life of radical openness and obedience of the Son Jesus to God his Father was Jesus' way to eventually know his Father, and thus to be able to reveal him further:

> All things have been delivered to me by my Father; and no one knows the Son except the Father, and no one knows the Father except the Son and anyone to whom the Son chooses to reveal him. (Matt. 11:27; see also Luke 10:22)

*Jesus as the Son of Man*
We have seen that Jesus understood his task as bringing in the active, reigning presence of God, his Father, and that he did this in his function as a humble and obedient Son, cost what it may. Just what did it cost him? This is best explained in terms of Jesus' claim to be the Son of Man. Again we are in an area of intense scholarly discussion, and I can only summarily report here the results of a long-time close association with this scholarship.

Jesus calls himself 'the Son of Man' over seventy times in the Gospels. Although many of these are parallels, where Matthew and Luke are merely repeating what was in Mark or their source, this strange term is used more than any other to speak of Jesus. What is even more extraordinary is the fact that *only* Jesus uses it, and always to speak of *himself*. It would seem that we have here a key to what Jesus thought of himself, but what does the term 'the Son of Man' mean?

It is here that scholars begin to argue, but I believe that it came to Jesus from his Jewish background, especially from Dan. 7:13. In the Book of Daniel Israel is being exhorted to trust in her faithful God through all of her sufferings, persecutions and death which she was experiencing when the book was written (about 165 B.C., at the same time as the stories in the Books of the Maccabees). The seventh chapter of the work is central to its whole argument. The message of Dan. 7 is one of encouragement. Great beasts (the persecutors of Israel) have arisen and caused suffering and death, especially the most recent tyrant (Antiochus IV from Syria). But if Israel would but hope and trust in her faithful God, she would have the last word. All the enemies would be destroyed, and Israel would be finally vindicated. This is what is promised in Dan. 7:13–14:

And behold with the clouds of heaven
    there came one like a son of man
and he came to the Ancient of Days
    and was presented before him.
And to him was given dominion
    and glory and kingdom . . .
His dominion is an everlasting dominion,
    which shall not pass away
and his kingdom one
    that shall not be destroyed.

When Jesus comes to take over the term, he no longer speaks of 'a son of man'. He applies it to himself as '*the* Son of Man'. Like the nation Israel in Dan. 7 ('one like a son of man'), he saw his life as a continual commitment to suffering, persecution and death. However, by taking over the term 'the Son of Man' he announced that his way of suffering, persecution and loss of self in love and service was not senseless. In fact, it gave sense and purpose to his life, as he went further and further into a mysterious future, full of trust, hope, love and obedience to the God of Israel. It was precisely because of his relationship of obedience as Son that his experience as the Son of Man made sense. He went on, not *knowing* all that stood before him, but in his obedience, *trusting* that God his Father would have the last word. And that was exactly how it happened: a death, yes; but followed by the saving and glorious intervention of God in the resurrection. Jesus, Son and Son of Man, was at the one time the most obedient and yet the most free human being that ever existed. He had no desire or need to *control* his future, as his radical obedience and trust in his Father freed him from all such concerns.

Here we have a Jesus we can follow. He was completely open to his Father in obedience, and that obedience gave him the freedom which led him away from himself into the strange loss of himself in love: an obedient suffering love that ultimately made sense in the resurrection. This is the way that all Christians are asked to go when they are asked to 'walk behind Jesus of Nazareth'. Jesus has done it, and he has thus become the first born from the death and slavery that sin and the desire to control the world have brought. Those who are prepared to follow Jesus, Son and Son of Man will follow him right through to the ultimate freedom that only resurrection can give. Only now can we begin to sense the centrality of obedience in the life of the Christian.

## Vatican II

The attitude of Jesus is taken as fundamental to the vow of obedience, and this is reflected in the Council document on the Religious life (*Perfectae Caritatis* 14). Once more one finds that the Council document uses traditional language, and there are several expressions to which people nowadays could react rather badly. Nevertheless, I believe that the traditional idea behind this number of the document still has a tremendous importance.

A first reading of the Council text will indicate why this is the case. The Council Fathers have used an abundance of biblical references, thus correctly founding this aspect of the vowed life on the life-style of Jesus.

> Through the profession of obedience, religious offer to God a total dedication of their own wills as a sacrifice of themselves; they thereby unite themselves with greater steadiness and security to the saving will of God.

This introductory statement is somewhat difficult for a generation of Religious who, quite correctly, do not see their lives of obedience as a loss of their uniqueness. However, the biblical section, which now follows, is very good:

> In this way they follow the pattern of Jesus Christ, who came to do the Father's will (cf. John 4:34; 5:30; Heb. 10:7; Ps. 39:9). 'Taking the nature of a slave' (Phil. 2:7), he learned obedience from his sufferings (cf. Heb. 5:8).

As can be seen from our earlier reflections on the Gospel picture of the obedient Jesus, the Council Fathers are close to the mark in this section of their document. The number goes on:

> Under the influence of the Holy Spirit, religious submit themselves to their superiors, whom faith presents as

God's representatives and through whom they are guided into the service of all their brothers in Christ.

Again we find the tendency to move back to an older way of expression. The reference to superiors, if understood in terms of the idea that they more or less have a 'hot line' to God, is widely rejected in many circles today. However, that is not the only way in which this expression can be understood, as we will see later. The number concludes by again correctly turning to the life-style of Jesus of Nazareth:

> Thus did Christ himself out of submission to the Father minister to the brethren and surrender His life as a ransom for many (cf. Matt. 20:28; John 10:14–18). In this way, too, religious assume a firmer commitment to the ministry of the Church and labour to achieve the mature measure of the fullness of Christ (cf. Eph. 4:13).

Although we find some of the older expressions in this Conciliar statement, also present is an all-important biblical model, insisting that the Religious, in professing obedience, is called to follow the life-style of Jesus of Nazareth. But once we have established that the imitation of Christ is where our obedience has its source, then we can see that my continual insistence throughout this book again comes to the fore: if a Religious must be obedient in imitation of Christ, then *all Christians* must be obedient. The Religious is not the only one who is called to imitate Christ, all the baptized are.

## Obedience: The Imitation of Christ

The Religious community is a microcosm of the Church: the Church in action, a visible, tangible group which we can call 'Church'. It exists because the people who make up that community believe in the salvation which comes to us through Jesus of Nazareth, the bringer of the Reign of God, Son of God and Son of Man. We have come here because of an experience of faith, and the goal of each one of us is to imitate the object of our faith as closely as possible – or to spend the rest of our lives working at it anyway! The immensity of that challenge can be gathered from the few pages which we have dedicated to a short portrait of the person of Jesus.

The fundamental need of a Religious committed to this life-style is to know Christ. How can one imitate a person if one does not know him? This I feel is one of the great problems of the Church and thus of Religious life. A recognition of the problem stands behind the Council's request that we return to the scriptures (*Perfectae Caritatis* 2). We hear so often: 'Come closer to Jesus; know Jesus; imitate Jesus, pray to Jesus.' But who is he? What does he mean to me? Does he remain that image which appealed to me as a teenager? Or have I grown in an understanding of the person and personality of this man? This is a very important series of questions which are often never posed. We must *know* Christ Jesus and not just commit ourselves to some fantasy or some attractive artistic presentation of him which strikes our fancy, but which can always be kept in a frame on a wall . . . well distant from the depths of me! A false, fanciful or unrealistic christology *necessarily* produces a false, fanciful or unrealistic Christianity. We must know Christ Jesus and have him continually before us, as we move further and further away from ourselves into him, because that is the only direction the knowledge of Christ can lead us. The more we grow, the more we will be prepared to cast off *our* ideas so that we might lose ourselves in the mystery of following Jesus, Son and Son of Man. This is a life of faith, and it is therefore the reason why we exist as a Religious community. The challenge of faith, however, must become real and vital and this will only happen when it becomes a *personal* challenge. Only when we are called into action or into a quality of life because of the impact of a personality upon us will the challenge really transform us. Unless the challenge of faith is real and personal, it becomes a chasing after pious rainbows.

This need was immediately recognized in the earliest Church. The earliest records we have of Christian communities are the letters of Paul and, as we will see, his whole theology of obedience and authority rests on the premise of the *personal* challenge to a life of faith. He could write to the Ephesians: 'Be imitators of God as beloved children'. This notion would not be new to people familiar with Jewish thought, as it was common to Hebrew thought to imitate God as a child would imitate a father – the perfect Israelite being understood as a son of God in so far as he was an obedient follower of the law of God. But Paul goes further, and speaks in more detail of the modality of that imitation: 'And walk in love, as Christ loved us and gave himself up for us, a fragrant offering and sacrifice to God' (Eph. 5:1–2). To be imitators of God sounds attractive, but how is this possible? The Ephesians are told that it is only possible through walking in love. Now, at least, we have something a little more concrete, but there are all sorts of activities called, rightly or wrongly, 'love'. Is there any further indication of how the Christian should love? A definite concrete model is offered: 'As Christ loved us'. The Church is no longer faced with the challenge of a God who was always present, but somehow never to be grasped, a God who revealed himself through battles, prophets and words, through times of famine and times of plenty. That was the Old Testament's preparation for the Christ event. Now he has become a personal encounter with a concrete historical figure called Jesus of Nazareth, and Paul asks that we imitate the way he loved. Jesus is the concrete example; to imitate

God, Christians have to love as Christ loved, that is, completely, in a radical obedience to God our Father.

However, even a slight knowledge of the situation of this community reveals another problem. How many people in Ephesus knew Jesus? For how many people in Ephesus did that appeal to Jesus and his gift of self in love represent a personal calling? Probably no one. Thus Paul must somehow render historical the Christ–Christian challenge. Paul was a realist; he was aware that one can talk on endlessly about love, but if the love that we believe in is the love that Christ showed us, then it must become a personal challenge, not merely something one talks about. To do this Paul took the only step possible, and in so doing laid the basis for all subsequent Christian authority: 'Be imitators of me, as I am of Christ' (1 Cor. 11:1). Paul presents himself as an historical, concrete presence in the community who demands obedience from them on the basis of the fact that he is presenting the demand of Christ to them. This extraordinary statement of Paul: 'Be imitators of me, as I am of Christ', has been explained away as an example of Paul's possible arrogance; Paul in a weak moment, when he has become a little 'big-headed', anxious to let his community know how good he was. However, all the letters of Paul written to communities who knew him personally contain similar statements (e.g. 1 Thess. 1:6; 1 Cor. 4:16–17; Gal. 4:12; Phil. 4:9). It would have been unrealistic of Paul to write to the Romans or to the Colossians: 'Be imitators of me . . .' because he had never been known by them as a physical, historical imitator of Christ in their midst.

As a matter of fact, this idea is not restricted to Pauline writings; the first letter of Peter contains something similar. Writing to the authorities of the community he says: 'Tend the flock of God that is in your charge not by constraint but willingly, not for shameful gain but eagerly, not as domineering over those in your charge but by being

an example to the flock. An example that merits imitation'
(1 Peter 5:2–3). As with Paul, the author is insisting that
authority is only to be had and exercised by one who
'willingly' and 'eagerly' is prepared to lead his flock by
example.

Paul's awareness that it was useless merely to preach
Christ is shown by the fact that he keeps coming back to
this principle. He knows that the only way he can claim
to have any authority is by insisting that he represents the
very presence of Christ in their midst. Perhaps the clearest
example of this comes at the end of the first chapter of
the letter to his beloved community at Philippi:

> For me to live is Christ, and to die is gain. If it is to be
> life in the flesh, that means fruitful labour for me. Yet
> which I shall choose I cannot tell. I am hard pressed
> between the two. My desire is to depart and be with
> Christ, for that is far better. But to remain in the flesh
> is more necessary on your account. Convinced of this,
> I know that I shall remain and continue with you all,
> for your progress and joy in the faith, so that *in me* you
> may have ample cause to glory *in Christ Jesus*, because
> of my coming to you again. (Phil. 1:21–6. See also
> 2:12–13)

The choice which Paul suggests that he has to make is a
rhetorical device, but it throws into great relief the need
for a 'fleshly', historical presence of the man Paul in the
community, so that they may find again the challenge of
the person and message of Jesus of Nazareth.

This Pauline solution of the problem of obedience and
authority is something that must go on through the ages.
A little reflection shows that it is the only way we can
hope to have valid authority in a Christian community.
We do not belong to economic communities, political
communities, football clubs, social clubs, or any other
form of secular community structure. We belong to a faith

community. How often errors are made here. There has been a great post-conciliar movement to democratize Religious life, but what is the guarantee that 'democracy' is what we need? Democracy is a form of government invented by the Greeks in the fifth century B.C. It may well work for us . . . but it must not become a new 'absolute', as it is a man-made system. Similarly, how often we have heard said over the chaos of some recent situations: 'If you were working in a bank and you were told to do such and such, then you would do it'. The answer, of course, is: 'I am not working in a bank. I belong to a faith community that has its sense and its unity because of our shared faith in Christ Jesus'. It is from this fact that we must work out our theology of obedience, and any 'system' which allows it to work will be valid. Any other foundation would be false. Our Christian communities are based on the Incarnation. I cannot stress this enough because it is here that, despite the somewhat traditional expressions used by the Council, its teaching remains valid.

The statement from the Council spoke of the superior's taking the place of God. I would find that impossible to accept if it meant that the superior was God on earth, with plenipotentiary powers over all men. It is not that the superior has a hot line to God, but that the authority figure renders incarnational, in a historical, flesh and blood concrete person, the call to be imitators of Christ. The Christian authority-figure has authority only in so far as he or she can repeat with Paul: 'Be imitators of me, as I am of Christ'!

What is being presented here as the ideal is not a new notion in the history of the Religious life. It stands at the heart of St Benedict's treatment of 'what kind of man the Abbot ought to be' in chapter 2 of his Rule. He wrote, for example: 'He is believed to hold the place of Christ in the monastery', and later he added: 'He should show forth all goodness and holiness by his deeds rather than his words'. It is also significant, in the light of our short reflections on the obedience of Jesus, that the word 'Abbot' comes from the expression 'Abba'.

To the extent that the authority-figure re-incarnates Christ, he has authority in a Christian community. This sounds very idealistic indeed, and puts the stress on the authority-figure, so two points need to be made very clearly at this stage.

First, no authority-figure re-incarnates Christ, as all are sinners. However, the ideal is that all authority-figures see their primary task, within the context of their community, as a continual attempt, through a quality of life, to act as a central figure reminding the people with whom and for whom they live of the values of Christ. The superior's task is to say to the community: 'Be imitators of me, as I am trying to be an imitator of Christ'.

Secondly, any authority-figure who tries to thus exercise authority without a community which understands his role and function in this way will soon come to grief. In other words, the ability for re-living the biblical model of Christian authority will be made possible only in a Christian community which shares that ideal. This is ultimately where a great number of experiments to live such a form of authority and obedience have failed. The superiors appointed have often done well, but the communities were not prepared to open themselves up to the risk of the radical life-style of Jesus of Nazareth. However, it was generally the superior who was blamed for the failure.

I believe that the Pauline ideal of authority in the community acts as a force to draw the community together, as an attempt to constitute the whole Christ. As someone earnestly strives on a full-time basis to present the community with the reality of the challenge of Jesus to each one of them to go further and further away from himself into the mystery of God, that person becomes the head towards whom all look in hope. This figure helps us to make sense of the everyday work in which we are involved, shows us that success at this level is not ultimately the touch-stone of our value to the community, and makes clear, not only in words but in his or her person and function within the community, what our life is really all about: a radical openness to God our Father, in imitation of Jesus, Son and Son of Man. Paul never speaks of obedience to the will of God and he never speaks of an obedience to a 'law'. He speaks only of obedience to Christ (2 Cor. 10:5–6) or to the Gospel (Rom. 10:16; Gal. 2:14; 5:7). These two (Christ and the Gospel) are, in reality, one and the same, as the preaching of the Gospel through word and quality of life is the continuation of the presence of Christ down through the centuries. Paul can thus speak of an obedience which is faith, an obedience which is a total commitment of the believer to the following of Christ.

We believe, along with St Irenaeus (who died about A.D. 180), that those of us who are prepared to let everything go and commit ourselves totally to Christ will ultimately be those people most fully alive: 'The glory of God is man fully alive' (*Adversus Haereses* IV, 20, 7). We are convinced that we will be fully Christian only when we are fully human. A fear-ridden individual who has to be protected from all decision-making by a strong superior, is not fully human and therefore not fully Christian. Another person who wants to do his or her 'own thing' all the time has lost the sense of the cross, of being an imitator of Christ who, 'though he was in the form of God, did not count equality with God a thing to be grasped, but emptied himself, taking the form of a servant' (Phil. 2:6–7). Such a person can hardly be called fully Christian, and therefore not fully human either. Thus the commitment to obedience becomes, ultimately, our means to the fullness of life, the fullness of Christianity, the fullness of humanity. Authority has the tremendously difficult task of creating a situation where this can happen: a situation where a Religious can make a fully human and a fully free decision to commit him or herself continually to the imitation of Christ. If this situation exists, by what right does a Religious refuse obedience? If it is lacking, by what right does the Religious superior ask for obedience?

## The Practice of Obedience

The radical nature of the biblical message is clear, but now, when we turn to look at the working out of this model of obedience in our lives, the difficulties arise. The message of the upward call into Christ (see Phil. 3:14) leaves totally free the individual's initiative and responsibility, but all of this has to be exercised within a context of a total dedication on the part of both the individual and the community to the continual imitation of Jesus of Nazareth. This, of course is very difficult to *control*, and thus open to criticism and it would be foolish to assert that in this situation mistakes will be avoided. While such a situation should produce many authentic decisions, it will not exclude the possibility of mistakes. As a rule we like to avoid mistakes; we prefer to have everything in order, under control all the time, and obedience has often been used by superiors as a weapon to make sure that this happens, by lopping off any initiative which may appear to be a threat to the established order. The Religious also used his obedience in the same way; he never ran the risk of making a mistake, as he could always claim to be acting under obedience. If anyone was at fault, it was the superior. Although this attitude to obedience has already been revised, and much progress has been made, it appears to me that we must go on with a re-assessment of the subject, and we need to work at renewal on two levels:

First, we need to review our attitude to the notion of superiors: who they are, how we choose them and what we expect from them. Behind this must stand the word of Jesus from the tenth chapter of Mark's Gospel:

> You know that those who are supposed to rule over the Gentiles lord it over them, and their great men exercise authority over them. *But it shall not be so among you;* but whoever would be great among you must be your servant, and whoever would be first among you must be slave of all. For the Son of Man also came not to be served but to serve, and to give his life as a ransom for many. (Mark 10:42–5)

This means, in practice, that many of the criteria which have been commonly used for the appointment of superiors should be revised. Often a superior is chosen because he or she has a strong personality, because he or she knows all about building construction, or is able to handle hospital administration, or a lay staff in a college, with skill. As is quite obvious, these criteria are used because the Religious life has been seen and understood as being primarily concerned with 'getting a job done', and the people best equipped to see to it are given authority, so that it might 'get done'. Given all that we have seen in our analysis of the vowed life, the primacy in the life of a Religious community must be shifted away from its being a work force into the challenge of the upward call into Christ. Surely 'the tasks' could be shared throughout the community, for a mutual enrichment and growth in our sense of shared responsibility. However, the responsibility for the challenge of a personal one-to-one encounter with the radical call to lose ourselves in love as we respond to the upward call into Christ cannot be reduced to a shared ideal. While the sharing of life and ideals in a genuine Christian community will always spur us on, since the event of the Incarnation the modality of the challenge has necessarily become a 'flesh and blood' experience. There must be a historical personality whose function in my life is to challenge me with the values and the life-style of Jesus of Nazareth.

Secondly, and perhaps more importantly, we need to undertake a renewal in ourselves, in our understanding of our life primarily as a life that makes sense because we belong to a faith community, and at the very centre of our lives should be a deep desire to be called further and further away from ourselves into the fullness of a life that can be had only in the imitation of Jesus of Nazareth.

If we can work at these two tasks then I believe that our obedience within our communities will become a sign in the world, a genuine instrument of evangelization where the members are seen to be maturely responsible, but totally dedicated to 'life in Christ'. The witness-value of our communities depends upon their being a setting where members make decisions regarding their own lives. The usual objections will be made that this leads to chaos and we must admit that this has, to a certain extent, happened. Far too often, however, we merely criticize and never come to grips with the real reasons why certain things have happened. One of the most important reasons for some of the chaos is that so many of us were trained in a certain form and understanding of obedience that we were too immature to adapt to the new presentation of obedience offered us by the Church and our own chapters. We either rejected it and withdrew from the risk of evangelical obedience, or abused our new-found freedom by behaving like children just let out of school. Now, fifteen years after the Council, another problem arises continually. In the 'unclear' period of the recent past many of us have firmly established ourselves in our little 'kingdoms', some of them outstanding works of charity which merit the praise of many. However, many of these 'kingdoms' and special apostolates are totally under our own *control*,

and we are loth to let go. A sincere imitation of the life-
style of Jesus of Nazareth must question all of this.

Any superior, even in a situation where the ideals outlined above are working, will on occasion have to act
authoritatively. There will be times when they will have
to intervene as Paul did when things were not going well.
We know that Paul gave a lot of specific directives; he was
well aware that he needed sometimes to enter a discussion
with severity. Some interesting facts emerge from a close
study of the Pauline interventions:

1. When Paul intervenes he does not do so on his own
authority, but to call his converts back to the Lord. For
example, he will continually indicate what comes from
the Lord and what is merely his own (see 1 Thess. 4:1–12;
1 Cor. 7:25). This shows very well where Paul bases his
authority. He is never issuing a call to life because of the
great knowledge or the intrinsic authority of Saul of Tar-
sus, but only in so far as he can call people to be imitators
of him as he is of Christ. The rest becomes relative.
2. Paul never makes the final decision. He presents a
teaching (the best example being the well-known case of
the incestuous relationship discussed in 1 Cor. 5), and
states what is to be done in the light of their new life in
Christ. He then leaves the matter to his community, and
the person involved must decide for or against the word,
person and teaching of Jesus. If he rejects Jesus, Paul has
no hesitation in recommending his expulsion from the
community, but even this is to be a salvific punishment,
'that his spirit may be saved in the day of the Lord Jesus'
(1 Cor. 5:5).

Rules and constitutions of Religious congregations and
the directives of superiors find their value here. They are
an attempt to re-incarnate and to re-present in a contemporary situation, the words, message and demands of Jesus
of Nazareth. Ultimately, this means that they are to call

the Religious to a life which is outstanding in the quality of its love. This was the way of Jesus of Nazareth, and it is the way his followers must go if they wish to show to the world that their obedience renders them authentically human, free to love.

Our earlier study of the obedience of Jesus did not produce some strange sort of character who was separated from our experience and thus distant from us. Jesus, like each one of us, experienced the whole gamut of human emotions and temptations. The difference between Jesus and us is that he never faltered in his obedience. Again the Letter to the Hebrews says it well: 'For we have not a high priest who is unable to sympathise with our weaknesses, but one who in every respect has been tempted as we are, yet without sin' (Heb. 4:15). Jesus' sinlessness did not arise from his being some sort of angelic being, but from his radical and never-failing obedience. We sometimes hear it said that the newer christologies have their value in showing that Jesus was human like us. That is not quite correct, as in his perfect obedience and his preparedness to go further and further away from himself in faith, hope and love, in his freedom to accept a future which God would create, Jesus alone was the *perfect* human being. He has made sense out of humanity, while we, in our sinfulness, egoism and selfishness, are always *less than human*. What is needed is that we become more and more human, as we move closer and closer to the quality of the life of love and obedience of Jesus of Nazareth, Son and Son of Man.

Returning to the working out of this within a concrete Religious community, and to the response of each member of a community, one must be realistic about the difficulties and tensions created by radical challenge to life and love. A situation where a superior decides every issue because of his or her insights or, worse still, because of some vested authority which gives power over the lives

and loves of others, must be avoided. We must continue
to reach decisions together. Many of us feel that the interminable community meetings, house councils and
provincial chapters have gone on for too long, and we are
weary of them. This is an understandable but dangerous
attitude. We must continue to face the hard work of these
interminable meetings, as only in this way can we hope
to come to some sort of light *together*. The way from
Pilate's praetorium to Golgotha must have also seemed
interminable to the cross-laden Jesus, but that journey led
to a resurrection. Nevertheless, there will always be some
situations where the superior will need to make decisions,
and these will cause anguish, pain, tears and real suffering.
There can be no realistic theology of obedience unless this
be taken into account. A painless theology of obedience
must be a false one. But if, behind these difficult situations, we have a community which is ultimately based on
love, then the problems which arise are not insurmount-
able. In a context of loving authority and loving obedience, no error on the part of superior or subject will be
irreparable, and this is another area where contemporary
Religious life needs to examine its conscience. A lack of
preparedness to accept error is a sign of a lack of love!


### The Function of the Vow of Obedience Today
The vowed life of obedience is touching the very heart of
the Christian response, as we all attempt to follow the
life-style of Jesus of Nazareth, Son and Son of Man, who
was totally directed by the will of God his Father, cost
what it may. All Christians are called to this form of life,
and they are not challenged by a mere 'idea', but by a
man, and since the Incarnation the Church has rendered
'incarnational', through all her fallible yet essentially human elements, the call to obedience. She has the mission
to present the challenge of the word and person of Jesus

of Nazareth to men and women of all ages in all their concerns.

Turning from the ideal to the signs of the times, there are two problems which I would simply like to point out.

1. The immediately obvious one that men and women (from the earliest times) tend to tear themselves away from God in a profound desire to *control*, to be the absolute masters of their own destiny. How well this tragedy is described already in the ninth century B.C., in Genesis 1—11. There is little need for me to list examples of the continued arrogance and egoism which is so much a part of our contemporary society, reflecting a deeply rooted movement away from the creating, calling Exodus God to whom man must not dictate terms, if he wishes to be truly human, truly all that God made him to be in the first place.

2. Closer to home we find a terrible danger within our own Church. As the historical, human institution of the Church is made up of men and structures, she will always be exposed to the risk of losing sight of the fact that she exists to call all men to 'life in Christ' through the ministry of Christ's word and sacrament. When the administration centres begin to think that they have the whole mystery of the life of Christ in his Church under their exclusive control, then the very sense of our existence as the Church founded by Christ is put into jeopardy. Little wonder that the Council spoke of the need for a Church which is 'at the same time holy and always in need of being purified' (*Lumen Gentium* 8).

Religious obedience is the obedience of a prophet. We must be seen as living under the divine urgency to go away from ourselves and to lose ourselves in the mysterious plan of a mysterious God. In this way we will continue to proclaim to the people among whom we live, the freedom which a radical openness to God can create, and we will act as a thorn in the side of an over-confident, over-organized, over-institutionalized Church, as the quality of our free but obedient lives will keep posing the question – Just why were you instituted in the first place?


## Conclusions

I believe that the so-called contemporary crisis of authority is a myth. The considerable amount of disarray we have experienced in the Religious life in recent years is not coming from a contempt for authority. I think that there is an innate feeling among people who read the Gospels that an authority which rules by law and rod is not Christian. What we want is real leadership, and that is hard to find and even harder to put into practice. We will never succeed unless we are all convinced that we are called to the one task: to reproduce in history a quality of a life of love which will make the world ask, 'What do these people have which makes them what they are? Why do we not have it?' When we have this quality of a life of love in our communities, then perhaps authority will have a real chance to lead us continually towards Christ. In any other situation, free, open and joint prayer-filled decision making is impossible, and the superior is swamped by the many bureaucratic requests which will inevitably have to be passed upwards, and he will be called upon continually to act as a referee in the many difficult situations and disputes which will always arise among us, but which should be resolved by the shared commitment to ultimate values of the people involved, without having to call upon higher authority.

We are living in an era of great opportunity and great light, and not in a time of crisis, but the responsibility for returning to an authority based upon Gospel values lies squarely on the shoulders of each one of us. The last Apostolic Exhortation of Pope Paul VI spoke about how

Religious evangelize. In many ways the Holy Father's
words sum up all that I have been trying to say: 'Religious,
for their part, find in their consecrated lives a privileged
means of effective evangelisation.' It is in our poverty,
chastity and obedience, in our consecrated lives, that we
find a privileged means of effective evangelization. How?
The late Pope goes on to explain how this functions:

> At the deepest level of their being they are caught up
> in the dynamism of the Church's life, which is thirsty
> for the divine absolute and the call to holiness. It is to
> this universal holiness that they bear witness. They
> embody the Church in her desire to give herself com-
> pletely to the radical demands of the Beatitudes. By the
> quality of their lives, they are a sign of total availability
> to God, the Church and the brethren. (*Evangelii Nun-
> tiandi* 69)

This will happen only if the lives of each one of us
commands respect and arouses questioning in the world
and among the people with whom we live. To do this we
have to be fully mature Christians, and our communities
exist to give us this opportunity. It will only happen,
however, if the ideal which calls this community into
existence, Jesus of Nazareth, is re-incarnated in the person
of the leader who is the symbolic centre without whom
true community in the Christian sense is impossible. But
the leader can only be so if the community governed is
totally concerned with the values of Christ; committed to
the task mapped out for us by the word of God:

> It is no longer we who live, but Christ who lives in us;
> and the life we now live in the flesh we live by faith in
> the Son of God, who loved us and gave himself for us.
> (see Gal. 2:20)

# FREE TO LOVE

The world in which we live out our vowed lives would laugh at the suggestion that a little book entitled 'Free to Love' could deal with such unfreeing things as poverty, chastity and obedience. I hope to have shown that the laughter comes from the world's inability to really understand freedom, and to really understand love.

There has only been one genuinely free person in the history of mankind: Jesus of Nazareth. His freedom arose from his profound openness to God, an openness which led him further and further away from the criteria of a worldly success story, into a human failure. It is here that the world is unable to see the real issue, because it will not admit its ultimate need for resurrection. Unable to go outside its categories of achievement and success-stories, things that can be measured in terms of human criteria and controllability, Jesus of Nazareth must be judged a failure. So also will it judge anyone who follows him along the same way of a total gift of self in love, a love which frees and does not possess, lit up only by the misty but powerful hope that this sort of love makes sense of life.

We hear on all sides that we are made slaves by our poverty, our chastity and our obedience. The problem which arises, however, is that many of us have allowed this criticism to develop by the poor quality of our lives of freedom and love. In some ways, we can tend to become slaves. To caricature a possible attitude: poverty means no money, chastity means no love and obedience means no decision making. Naturally, we scoff when we hear the vowed life spoken of in that way, but is there not a grain of truth in it? Are there not many among us who are looking for the wrong kind of freedom: a freedom from the responsibility of loving and being loved? Is this not slavery? It is my experience that there are many Religious in this situation, and most of us, when it suits, are prepared to lean on that particular crutch, no matter how eloquently our conferences and publications may speak of the need for a contrary approach to the Religious life.

How has this happened? The answer must be found by returning to the matter which I raised in the Preface. We have lost touch with the supreme norm of all Christian life: Jesus of Nazareth as he is portrayed in the Gospels. To be sure, there is a great deal of christological debate going on among the scholars, with all sorts of aggressive assertions and counter-assertions providing good press for *Time Magazine*. All this in the name of Jesus of Nazareth! But what of the everyday Christian who cannot even afford to purchase Küng, Schillebeeckx, Rahner and Kasper; let alone understand them when they read them? They are subjected to the ravings and the rantings of the various defenders of either the new thought or the old, and what is happening to the vital life-giving presence of the challenge of Jesus of Nazareth in the meantime?

There are many reasons why the Religious life is an all-important feature of the contemporary Church. Some of them I have already attempted to clarify in *Disciples and Prophets*. Here I would like to point out again that through all the polemics and confusion, the Church needs to be questioned by the quality of the life of a free and loving group of people in her midst, which sees its *primary task* as the continuation of the free and loving life-style of Jesus of Nazareth. Our poverty, our chastity and our obedience are not privileged possessions which set us apart from the Church and the rest of the world. Biblical poverty, chastity and obedience are the vocation of every man and woman, and they are, I hope I have indicated, our way to authentic humanity. It must be so, as through such a life-style we follow the poor, chaste and obedient Jesus along a path which leads to the ultimate answer to the deepest longings of the hearts of all men and women: resurrection. For many years J. M. R. Tillard has been insisting that the Religious life must accept as its 'project' the public living out, not just of an externally observed poverty, chastity and obedience, but the Gospel in its entirety. This is the only way in which we will announce to the world, by the quality of our lives already lived in the joy of the risen Christ, the freedom which produces genuine love.

More than that one cannot say, or ever hope to say. The world will continue to ask: 'What is freedom?' and even more insistently: 'What is love?', but the answer will not be found on the lips of the philosophers. It can only be found by looking again to Jesus of Nazareth, and by taking the risk of reproducing that same freedom and that same love in our own lives, as we follow him down his way. Why can we do no more? Why is it impossible to be more explicit about the exact nature of this freedom and this love? William H. Vanstone provides the answer:

> We are describing not that which any man has known or experienced but that towards which every man, at the depths of his being which is more profound than language, gropes and aspires. (*Love's Endeavour, Love's Expense*, pp. 53–4)

# A SELECT BIBLIOGRAPHY

With this short list I would like to indicate a few further books which have guided me, and which an interested reader may also find helpful.

Metz, J. B., *Followers of Christ: The Religious Life and the Church*. London, Burns and Oates, 1978.

Moloney, F. J., *Disciples and Prophets: A Biblical Model for the Religious Life*. London, Darton, Longman and Todd, 1980.

Murphy-O'Connor, J., *Becoming Human Together*. Dublin, Veritas, 1977.

Murphy-O'Connor, J. and others, *What is Religious Life? A Critical Reappraisal*. Dublin, Dominican Publications, 1977.

Raguin, Y., 'Chastity and Friendship', *Supplement to the Way* 19 (1973), 105–17.

Rahner, K., *Religious Life Today*. London, Burns and Oates, 1977.

Rees, D. and Others, *Consider your Call: A Theology of Monastic Life Today*, London, SPCK, 1978.

Tillard, J. M. R. *The Gospel Path: The Religious Life*. Bruxelles, Lumen Vitae, 1977.

Tillard, J. M. R., *There are Charisms and Charisms: The Religious Life*. Bruxelles, Lumen Vitae, 1977.

Wilcken, J., *Religious Life Today: A Theological and Scriptural Approach*. Melbourne, Polding Press, 1974.

Williams, H. A., *Poverty, Chastity and Obedience: The True Virtues*. London, Mitchell Beazley, 1975.

Vanstone, W. H., *Love's Endeavour, Love's Expense: The Response of Being to the Love of God*. London, Darton, Longman and Todd, 1977.

# Index of Biblical References

## Old Testament

# Index of Biblical References

## New Testament